On the Way to Heaven

On the Way to Heaven

A Christian's Individual Road Map

Gail Erwin Hale

ISBN-13: 9781542727280
ISBN-10: 1542727286

Cover design: Michal Taylor-Phillips
Interior sketches: Michal Taylor-Phillips
Back cover author photo: Susan Crutchfield Photography
Author biography: Rebekah Hale

Without my spiritual awakening of progressive sanctification truth thanks to Donna Stamey Carver, this book would never have been written.

The Lord Jesus Christ and His extraordinary gift of my salvation through His blood has made this book possible.

Table of Contents

Acknowledgments

The following people are to be thanked and appreciated for their contribution toward the completion of this book:

Donna Stamey Carver, whose dedication and service to the Lord, as a teacher and friend, directed my course of study regarding the nation of Israel and the Body of Christ as they relate to our progressive sanctification.

Maria I. Morgan, who has been an encourager and prayer warrior from the genesis of the book. Thank you for your initial guidance and invaluable directives regarding the components of publishing, marketing, and formatting of the manuscript.

Jenny Shumake, for faithful prayer and encouragement over the past year, as well as proofreading the finished manuscript of the book. Your suggestions and comments helped to progress the writing of the book to keep me moving forward toward my goal.

Kelly Bulger, for her likeminded friendship in the Lord and gracious editing skills demonstrated while proofreading the completed manuscript. Your wisdom and love for our Lord is always such an encouragement to me.

Bette Schumann, for her willingness to consider illustrating this book, followed by her recognition that God had not called her to serve in that capacity. Thank you for your suggestion of calling Michal to pursue her possible illustration of the book.

Michal Taylor-Phillips, for her sensitivity to the Lord's leading in using her gift of illustration to achieve the exact portrayal of Heather and Alice on the cover on their way to a glorious heaven, and the wisdom for the interior sketch of the tree hugging the Bible in its roots. Your suggestion of limiting the number of sketches was very instrumental in moving the book forward.

Timothy Male, my publishing consultant, and several others at CreateSpace who took me by the hand and guided me through the self-publishing process with patience and understanding, while being bombarded by my myriad of questions.

My husband, Melvin, whose encouragement and patience freed me up to spend many hours in my library and on my computer writing, editing, and rewriting each chapter of the book. You, who know me best, next to my Savior, were able to comfort me on those days when the writing process did not function according to expectations.

My daughter Susan Crutchfield, who took an afternoon out of her very busy schedule for a photo shoot and logged many hours examining the proofs and editing them to obtain just the right picture for my book cover.

My daughter Rebekah Hale, who took an outline of my engrossed life and transformed it into a complementary biosketch to assist the reader in knowing me better.

My other daughters, Jennifer Holman, Rachel Hale, and Piper Hale, who were very encouraging and listened to me talk about the progression of my book with great comments and suggestions.

Many friends and brothers and sisters in the Lord who prayed for me and inquired frequently during the past year how the book was progressing. I say thank you for your faithfulness and evidence of God's love to assist me in pressing on to finish this calling of the Lord.

Most of all, to my Lord and Savior, Jesus Christ, who saved me, had a plan for my progressive sanctification to bring forth maturity and wise discernment, and gave me a vision to write this book for His glory and the edification of its future readers.

Preface

Trust in the LORD with all thine heart; and lean not unto thine own understanding. In all thy ways acknowledge him, and he shall direct thy paths.

–PROVERBS 3:5–6

I never thought that I would be writing this book. Over the past thirty-three years, I have been teaching the Word of God to children in church ministry, to my five children in homeschool, to women one on one in person or on the telephone, to large groups of women with varied doctrinal backgrounds, and now for the past two years, to women weekly in a health and rehabilitation center.

My main focus has always been to teach the truth of God's Word that the apostle Paul described in 2 Timothy as "rightly dividing." Studying the Scripture for a long period of time does not necessarily ensure spiritual comprehension or beholding of the truth as God imparts it to His Body of Christ. The transformation of this truth into our daily walk with the Lord is a work accomplished by the Holy Spirit.

I have dedicated this book to my first proximal teacher of a few women, as differentiated from my first stadium-style teacher of many women. I am very thankful to the ministry of the large organizational Bible study where I actually met the Lord thirty-seven years ago, as well as the subsequent grounding in the great doctrinal truths found in the book of Romans. I began to identify my conversion with the apostle Paul's, minus the actual killing of Christians. My horrendous sin had been the verbal abuse and ridicule of God's people. The similarity with Paul was in the 180-degree repentance that resulted in an immediate external transformation of my outward behavior. My inner man, of course, continues to be transformed and renewed, and will be until I go home to be with my Lord.

After almost a year of being immersed in an inductive study of the foundational book of Romans, my whole life was being transformed by the continual renewing of my mind, from the intellectualism that had defined me to a freedom and peace that I never dreamed existed. I could not study enough, but the Lord reminded me that I had a husband and young daughter, and He reined me in to a more balanced life. At this point in time, I did not know that God was preparing me to be a teacher of His Word. In order to teach the Bible, we need to have the Word of Christ "dwelling in us richly" so that we may know how to "answer every man."

At this juncture in my life, I began attending a Bible study under the direction of Donna Stamey, now Carver, and found inexhaustible treasures in God's Word that began to define the "new me" and direct my focus of study. The details are too numerous to describe for the purposes of this preface, but suffice it to say that my perspective of studying the nation of Israel compared to the Body of Christ, illuminated the Word of God and its eternal purposes that continues to direct my path of inductive Bible study and teaching.

Initially God directed me to teach children in summer backyard Bible studies, in an organized ministry to children, and of course, vacation Bible school. I was also homeschooling my own five daughters, with the Bible as the center of their education. We used a well-respected curriculum that correlated each subject with the Word of God, as well as using the same vocabulary and concepts among the different subjects of English, math, science, and so on. I was learning in great detail along with my children, and this continued to augment the spiritual maturity and wisdom in my life. As a family, we were used for a brief time to minister to the children of battered and abused women, while their mothers attended a Bible study. My eyes were truly opened when I began teaching about Adam and Eve and the fall and one of the older children asked, "Who?"

God began using my gifts at this period of time in my life to teach other Christian women one on one at the level of spiritual wisdom the Holy Spirit had led me to behold. Often, a woman would call me on the phone with a "quick question" that would morph into several hours of discussion.

From here, the Bible studies grew to more women and various settings, including devotions for brides-to-be, baby showers, and home-school seminars. The Lord was shaping my doctrinal beliefs and giving me a firm foundation to feel "at home" in His Word.

All of these preliminaries are to emphasize the passage of time that the progressive sanctification process entails in order to produce maturity in a teacher of God's Word.

The spiritual growth never is complete until we are at home in heaven with the Lord.

Two years ago, I had a strong desire to begin writing a book on the spiritual growth of a believer. I actually wrote the first chapter and was unable to proceed at that time. Last year, the desire to continue with the book became even stronger. I knew that God was giving me a gift to write a compilation of the truth He had placed within my "inner man" for His glory, and to encourage and instruct other Christian women on their individual journeys with the Lord. That, in essence, is the purpose of this book that you are now reading. I prayed for each of you as I joyfully labored by the direction and grace of God over the past year. I have compared this process to labor and delivery of a child, because I see them both as a wonderful miracle brought forth by the divine providence of God.

If the Lord uses this book in your life to open up your eyes of understanding, to produce changes in your relationship with Him, or to bring joy and encouragement to your personal walk, please contact me so I may rejoice with you.

Gail Erwin Hale
2017
Website: GailErwinHale.com

Explanations for
Understanding the
Format of this Book

In order to appreciate the essence of the scope of this book, a few explanations are necessary.

1. The Scriptures are all taken from the 1769 Cambridge edition of the King James Version of the Holy Bible: King James Version.

2. Scriptures from the New Testament that quote an Old Testament Scripture are written in all capital letters.

3. Several of the Scriptures are written out in their entirety.

4. Other Scriptures are just referenced to maintain succinctness of the text and to encourage the reader to explore the Scriptures independently as the Holy Spirit leads.

5. The Scriptures presented to support various concepts throughout the book are in no way exhaustive, but selected to embody the area of truth being examined at the time.

6. In several of the Scriptures there are words in parentheses that reflect the original Greek meanings and are presented to clarify the meaning. Often the words in the King James Version are not always defined in today's dictionaries in the same way as when the Bible was written in 1611. You are encouraged to refer to the original Greek meanings of words to facilitate your understanding of a questionable context.

7. All Greek words, as defined when Scriptures are examined and the verb tenses are expanded, are taken from Spiros Zodhiates, *The Complete Word Study New Testament King James Version* (AMG, 1991). The Greek words are italicized and the meanings are in quotation marks.

1

My Perspective on Teaching God's Word

All Scripture is given by inspiration of God and is profitable for doctrine for reproof, for correction, for instruction in righteousness.

−2 TIMOTHY 3:16

Study to show thyself approved unto God, a workman that needeth not to be ashamed, rightly dividing the word of truth.

−2 TIMOTHY 2:15

I believe you should know my perspective about teaching the Word of God to facilitate your understanding of my observation and interpretation of Scripture as related to the presentation of biblical truths in this book. The two Scriptures from the book of 2 Timothy in the heading above define the spectrum of my teaching approach.

To understand the implications of these two Scriptures some background information is necessary. The book of 1 Timothy was written about AD 63 from Macedonia, as supported in 1 Timothy 1:3: "As I besought thee to abide still at Ephesus, when I went into Macedonia, that thou mightest charge some that they teach no other doctrine." The appointed time of this book's writing was following the apostle Paul's release from house arrest in Rome at the end of the book of Acts.

The book of Titus was written about AD 65 from Macedonia or from Nicopolis for the purpose of encouragement to Titus as we read in Titus 3:12, "When I shall send Artemas unto thee, or Tychicus, be diligent to come unto me to Nicopolis: for I have determined there to winter."

The book of 2 Timothy was written about AD 66 from the apostle Paul's second Roman imprisonment after he had been taken prisoner at Troas. This location is supported in 2 Timothy 4:13, "The cloak that I left at Troas with Carpus, when thou comest, bring with thee, and the books, but especially the parchments." At that time Paul was about to be beheaded, and this imminence is penned by Paul in 2 Timothy 4:6, "For I am now ready to be offered, and the time of my departure is at hand."

The relevant context of the book of 2 Timothy is as follows:

1. To continue to stand fast as a soldier for Christ (2:3)
2. Warnings of signs of the last days (3:1–9)
3. Exhortations for preaching the Word (4:1–5)
4. End of the life of a true soldier (4:6–8)

Philippians 1:21–24, a cross-reference written in AD 61, further defines the mind-set of Paul regarding his ministry and rest in the Lord.

The last book the apostle Paul wrote before his death was 2 Timothy. Paul was at the height of his maturity while writing this book, so these Scriptures become important to scrutinize. The tone of 2 Timothy becomes one of exhortation and encouragement as the apostle Paul passes the baton to his protégé Timothy.

Six components of exhortation may be considered when interpreting a scripture:

- teaching
- a reminder
- encouragement
- to commend
- a warning
- correction

Let's begin with a look at *teaching*. With an initial teaching, a person is hearing the truth for the first time, which is supported by the Scripture Genesis 2:16–17: "And the Lord God commanded the man, saying, Of every tree of the garden thou mayest freely eat. But of the tree of knowledge of good and evil, thou shalt not eat of it: for in the day that thou eatest thereof thou shalt surely die."

Next, we examine a *reminder*. This infers that the truth has been heard before, and is corroborated by Philippians 3:1: "Finally my brethren, rejoice in the Lord. To write the same things to you, to me is not grievous, but for you it is safe."

We need to consider *encouragement,* which is to tell someone to keep on doing what they are already doing, and is validated by Colossians 1:23, "If ye continue in the faith grounded and settled and be not moved away from the hope of the gospel, which ye have heard, and which was preached to every creature which is under heaven; whereof I Paul is made a minister."

The fourth component is to *commend,* to tell people who are doing well in the Lord to keep on going, which is supported by 1 Timothy 4:6: "If thou put the brethren in remembrance of these things, thou shalt be a good minister of Jesus Christ, nourished up in the words of faith and of good doctrine, whereunto thou hast attained."

The fifth component is *a warning,* a preventative measure directing one to be vigilant, as described in Colossians 2:8: "Beware lest any man spoil you through philosophy and vain deceit, after the tradition of men, after the rudiments of the world, and not after Christ."

The last component is *correction,* which is to stop what you are now doing as Paul described in 1 Corinthians 1:10–11: "Now I beseech you, brethren, by the name of our Lord Jesus Christ, that ye all speak the same thing, and that there be no divisions among you; but that ye be perfectly joined together in the same mind and in the same judgment. For it hath been declared unto me of you, my brethren, by them which are of the house of Chloe, that here are contentions among you."

In the Old Testament, there are commands according to the law with immediate consequences. The book of Leviticus is replete with specific commands related to the law of God and the impending consequences when a particular law is disobeyed. The boundaries and infractions are described in Leviticus 20: 7–9: "Sanctify yourselves therefore, and be ye holy: for I am the Lord your God. And ye shall keep my statutes and do them: I am the Lord which sanctify you. For every one that curseth his father or his mother shall be surely put to death: he hath cursed his father or his mother, his blood shall be upon him." There are several conditional *if-then* statements in the Old Testament related to the nation of Israel. For example, Jeremiah 31:36: "*If* those ordinances depart from before me, saith the Lord, *then* the seed of Israel also shall cease from being a nation from before me forever." A requirement for restoration and confession is contained in Leviticus 26:40–42: "*If* they shall confess their iniquity, and the iniquity of their fathers, with their trespass which they trespassed against me, and that also they have walked contrary unto me: And that I also have walked contrary unto them, and have brought them into the land of their enemies; *if* then their uncircumcised hearts be humbled, and they then accept of the punishment of their iniquity: *Then* will I remember my covenant with Jacob, and also my covenant with Abraham will I remember: and I will remember the land."

The primary focus of the New Testament is grace, as demonstrated by the Crucifixion of the Lord Jesus Christ for all who are born into sin, 1 Timothy 1:15: "Christ Jesus came into the world to save sinners." When a person becomes a believer by faith in the death, burial, and resurrection of Jesus Christ, he is a new creature. As a new Christian, this person now possesses all the spiritual blessings; Ephesians 1:3: "Blessed be the God and Father of our lord Jesus Christ, who hath blessed us with all spiritual blessings in heavenly places in Christ."

With the focus on grace, there is unconditional love that does not require the conditional declarations of *if-then* as described in the Old Testament. The only *if-then* is, *if* you are in a relationship with Christ Jesus the Lord, *then* you have all the spiritual blessings given by God unconditionally.

In the pre-Pauline books of the Bible, there are several commands as related to the nation of Israel. The apostle Paul, however, teaches the previously expounded definitions of exhortation mainly in the prison epistles of Ephesians, Philippians, and Colossians. The definition of "exhortation" is "to encourage and strengthen." Also included in the definition is "to continue on the way you are going, beseech, implore, advise." All of these words convey a tenderness, not harshness, such as a military command. The Greek word for exhortation is *paraklesis.* 1 Timothy 4:13 states, "Till I come, give attendance to reading, to exhortation, to doctrine."

Other New Testament references for exhortation include Romans 12:8, "Or he that exhorteth, on exhortation"; 1 Corinthians 14: 3, "But he that prophesieth speaketh unto men to edification, and exhortation, and comfort"; 2 Corinthians 8:17, "For indeed he accepted the exhortation; but being more forward, of his own accord he went unto you"; and 1 Thessalonians 2:3, "For our exhortation was not of deceit, nor of uncleanness, nor in guile."

Keeping the setting, purpose, and style of Paul's approach to conveying sound doctrine in 2 Timothy, the two selected Scriptures appear to cover the spectrum of completeness in teaching the Word of God. Let's unpack and inspect these two Scriptures to determine how they define a part of the entire comprehensiveness of interpreting God's Word.

Beginning with 2 Timothy 3:16, "All Scripture is given by inspiration of God and is profitable for doctrine for reproof, for correction, for instruction in righteousness," we see that all scripture is given by inspiration of God. Simply put, that means from Genesis to Revelation, every single scripture was inspired or "God breathed." The actual Greek word for "given by inspiration of God" is *theopneustos* or "divinely breathed," and it only occurs in 2 Timothy 3:16 in the New Testament. The word "and" in the Greek is *kai* which means "and so" and acts as a cumulative force indicating to keep going forward.

Paul describes all Scripture as profitable for doctrine. "Profitable" in the Greek is *ophelimos*, which means "helpful, serviceable, advantageous, useful." This word is used two other times in the New Testament: 1 Timothy 4:8, "For bodily exercise profiteth little: but godliness is profitable unto all things, having promise of the life that now is, and of that which is to come"; and Titus 3:8, "This is a faithful saying, and these things I will that thou affirm constantly, that they which have believed in God might be careful to maintain good works. These things are good and profitable unto men." The Greek word *didaskalia* means "instruction" or "teaching." We infer from this initial perusal that every Scripture in the Bible is not only inspired by God, but is profitable, "helpful, serviceable, useful" (Greek word *ophelimos*) for instruction or teaching.

The doctrine or teaching highlighted in 2 Timothy 3:16 is for reproof, for correction, and for instruction in righteousness. "Reproof" is the Greek word *elegchos*, which means "conviction, proof, evidence." As we are studying the Scriptures, individually or in a group, conviction regarding an area of our lives often occurs. This conviction may be related to an ongoing sin, an attitude, or a direction God is leading us to pursue. The actual conviction is not from self-effort, but the work of the Holy Spirit, using God's Word to transform our minds into truth. According to 2 Corinthians 3:18, "But we all with open face beholding in a glass the glory of the Lord are changed from glory to glory even as by the spirit of the Lord."

Refer to chart 1 in the appendix ("Summary of Verse Analysis on 2 Corinthians 3:18") to assist you in the understanding of the great importance of this verse for the believer's beholding of spiritual growth. Take the time to study each grouping of words comprising this verse in order to extract the individual components that aggregate to explain exactly how we walk in "new-ness of life."

The overview of 2 Corinthians 3:18 with a succinct rendering is that it is written to people who have put their trust in the Lord Jesus Christ for salvation; are actually understanding the glory of the Lord as defined by the character of God; are changed in a miraculous way when studying the Scriptures, from glory of deep-rooted truth to glory resulting in evidential manifestation of fruit in the believer during progressive sanctification; and all by the transformation accomplished by the Holy Spirit. This Scripture, with an emphasis on the glory of the Lord, will be examined further in chapter 7.

The next area of teaching is *correction*, which is the Greek word *epanorthosis* used only in 2 Timothy 3:16. The meaning of *epanorthosis* is "straightening up again, rectification, reformation, improvement of life and character." As we walk through our Christian life, we may stray off the path a bit into an area that in itself is not incompatible with the teaching of God's Word, but may be harmful to us individually. For instance, in Romans Paul addressed the weaker and stronger brother as related to Christian liberty. In chapter 14, Paul is discussing the eating of meat that may have been sacrificed to idols and the keeping of holy days; both were offenses to the immature believers who wanted to continue to keep the law. Paul's answer was given in Romans 14:13–14: "Let us not therefore judge one another any more: but judge this rather, that no man put a stumbling block or an occasion to fall in this brother's way. I know, and am persuaded by the Lord Jesus, that there is nothing unclean of itself: but to him that esteemeth any thing to be unclean, to him it is unclean."

Instruction in righteousness is divided into the Greek words *paldeia* for "instruction," *en* for "in," and *dikaiosune* for "righteousness." *Paldeia* is defined as "education, training, or nurture." The essence of this word is in training up a child, disciplining by punishment, leading, or teaching. The word *en* is defined as "position in place, time, or state." *Dikaiosune* is defined as "equity of character or act, Christian justification, right action: a gracious gift of God to men whereby all who believe on the Lord Jesus Christ are brought into a right relationship with God." This righteousness is unattainable by obedience to any law, or merit of man's own, or any other condition. With the combination of the words "instruction in righteousness," we see that as believers we learn the truth by God's gracious gift of salvation through Jesus Christ to restore our fellowship in a right relationship with God and not by an attempt to keep the law. Two Scriptures that support this definition are Philippians 3:6, "Concerning zeal, persecuting the church: touching the righteousness which is the law blameless," and Philippians 3:9, "be found in him, not having mine own righteousness, which is of the law, but that which is through the faith of Christ, the righteousness which is of God by faith." Prior to conversion, Paul believed that he was doing the Lord's work by keeping the law, but as he matured in the faith following salvation on the road to Damascus, he understood that righteousness is found only in a relationship with the Lord Jesus Christ.

In summary, 2 Timothy 3:16 tells us that all of God's Word is "God breathed" as the human author of each book pens through divine guidance, and is advantageous for teaching the believer, correction in the believer's life, and education and nurturing in right action by the believer through a gracious gift of God.

Now turning to 2 Timothy 2:15, "Study to show thyself approved unto God, a workman that needeth not to be ashamed, rightly dividing the word of truth," we can see that Paul exhorts us to "study" the Word, which is the Greek work *spoudazo*, meaning "to use, speed to, make effort, hasten to do a thing, exert oneself, and give diligence." The grammatical verb tense "for study" is the aorist imperative active; the aorist imperative denotes a command, request, or entreaty and does not involve a continuous or repetitive action. Instead, it is often used for general exhortations and for things that must be begun at that very moment.

Paul's great concern for Timothy and all believers was to emphasize the importance of digging into the Word. "To show" is the Greek word *paristemi*, which means "to stand beside or exhibit." The believer's approval, or *dokimos*, of God means "to be acceptable or tried." God, or *Theos*, is the Supreme Divinity. The word *Theos* is used in the New Testament as a direct reference to God. *Theos* is appropriated by the Jews and retained by Christians to denote the one true God.

"Workman" from the Greek word *ergates* translates into "laborer, worker, and teacher." The teacher of God's Word needs to know the Scriptures and their interpretation. *Anepaischuntos* translates into "that needeth not be ashamed" and literally means "no cause for shame." As you continue to study the Word, answers to the questions other people may ask you will be provided by the Holy Spirit, bringing forth the truth from the recesses of your renewed mind and heart.

The most important words in 2 Timothy 2:15 for a student of God's Word are "rightly dividing," or *orthotomeo* in the Greek. The meaning of this word is "to make a straight cut, dissect or expound correctly the divine message." Also, "handling aright, further cutting or dividing in a more general sense of rightly dealing with a thing." The word *orthotomeo* does not mean dividing Scripture from Scripture, but *teaching the scripture accurately*. Imagine for a moment telling one child to divide a cupcake and the other to distribute the cupcake. The child dividing the cupcake will certainly have two equal halves for his sibling to share. The Word of God must be interpreted accurately as God has inspired each Scripture to avoid being led into false doctrine, or not extracting from the Bible the exact truth that equips one for an abundant life of ministry and service to the Lord.

The rest of the verse tells us that the "word," or *logos*, is that which is rightly divided. *Logos* means "something said including the thought, topic of discourse, motive, the expression of thought, a saying or statement by God." And it is not just the word alone, but the word of truth. "Truth" is translated from *aletheia*, which means "reality lying at the basis of appearance, the manifested veritable essence of a matter, especially of Christian doctrine."

In summary, 2 Timothy 2:15 exhorts a Christian to study the Word of God, demonstrating his level of maturity attained to God, as a student that needs not be ashamed for lack of knowledge, teaching the Scripture accurately as God's Words that are reality and the essence of Christian doctrine.

Merging 2 Timothy 3:16 and 2 Timothy 2:15, I believe that every Scripture from Genesis to Revelation originates from God as He imparted them to man. All Scripture is useful for teaching in conviction, improvement of life and character, and education or training through a personal relationship with God through Jesus Christ as a gift from God but we must also study the Scriptures and teach them accurately as the truth of our Christian doctrine.

One example of this merging of 2 Timothy 3:16 and 2 Timothy 2:15 may help clarify the essence of this truth. If you go to the post office, you will find that there are many letters in the boxes. The letters are not all for you, just the ones in your box. Likewise, the Word of God contains sixty-six books that were all written by men under the inspiration of God. The books do not all pertain to each of us. We see the nation of Israel and animal sacrifices, which only were a covering for sin. We see the blood of Christ on the cross, which was the acceptable sacrifice for sin. Then we see the mystery revealed during Paul's ministry that Jew and Gentile are one and come to salvation through Jesus Christ the same way.

Even though the entire Bible does not relate directly to each individual, we will learn from all of it. How much more precious is the grace of God to us today when we read in the Old Testament about the intricate worship required by God through the specifications of the temple construction, each instrument of worship, and the various animal sacrifices to cover the sins of the nation of Israel.

Questions for Group Discussion or Individual Study

1. When examining the two scriptures from 2 Timothy 3:16 and 2:15, why is it important to know when 1 Timothy and Titus were written and from where they were written?

2. Review the context of the book of 2 Timothy by studying the Scriptures listed next to each of the four delineated topics of the book. Discuss the importance of each point of context and how it relates to your life and the condition of our world today.

3. Review the six components of exhortation and study the examples provided from Scripture. Discuss any personal examples of each type of exhortation from your own life, from a friend's life, or a relative's experience.

4. Do you understand the difference between the commands of the law as presented in the Old Testament compared to the exhortations of Paul as presented in his epistles? Look for other if-then statements. Then look at other examples of exhortations in the writings of Paul.

5. Examine 2 Timothy 3:16 and state the meaning of this Scripture in your own words.

6. Examine 2 Timothy 2:15 and state the meaning of this Scripture in your own words.

7. Do you believe these two Scriptures combine to explain how to study the Bible? Why or why not? Explain your conclusion in detail.

8. Was this description of my perspective for teaching God's Word clarifying enough to assist in the further reading of the book? Explain how it is or isn't helpful.

9. For further study look up Scriptures describing the nation of Israel in the Old Testament and the mystery as described by the apostle Paul in the New Testament.

10. An exhaustive concordance containing every word in the Bible is very helpful for studying the Hebrew and Greek meanings of the words. For an even more comprehensive study of grammar, cross-references, and expansion of word meanings, refer to Spiros Zodhiates, *The Complete Word Study New Testament King James Version* (AMG, 1991).

2

Christian Growth

Not by works of righteousness, which we have done, but according to his mercy he saved us, by the washing of regeneration, and renewing of the Holy Ghost

–Titus 3:5

Christian growth is one of the most misunderstood biblical truths in our churches today. Do we obey a set of rules? Do we just wait for God to show us what to do? Do we pull ourselves up by our own bootstraps? Or do we delve into the Word of God to find the answers? Think for a moment about your answer to each of these questions and how you would respond in your particular life situations. So many different interpretations of Scripture regarding spiritual growth exist in our churches today. Which one should you believe, and how do you know that the one you are following is correct?

This second chapter focuses on two Christian women living life in a way that is very unique to each one's situation and calling. They will be developed as characters to personify two different levels of spiritual growth. Throughout the book, they will be woven into some of the chapters for clarification of and identification with the developing concept of Christian growth.

Alice Buffington and Heather Cook

Characteristics:

Alice: Her focus is on service for the Lord as He leads in her daily life, not on what the Lord is doing for her. She is of medium height, with light brown hair in a trim pageboy style and bright blue eyes that are kind, compassionate, and shining with the Lord's light. Alice dresses modestly but neatly and uses color from her wardrobe to accent her face and hair, rather than excessive makeup. Always displaying a great sense of humor, Alice loves classical and Christian music, aesthetic poetry, reading the Bible and books of various literary genres, walking along nature trails meditating upon God's wondrous creation, and studying the Bible extensively to prepare for teaching and counseling women. Having walked with the Lord for several years, Alice beholds the sovereignty of God and boldly proclaims the truth of the Bible accompanied by the fruit of love which is daily manifested by serving others. She is not judgmental, but caring and considerate, knowing that God is the true judge. When interacting with people, Alice is usually able to discern an individual's level of maturity, which enhances her ability to minister for the Lord. Through many diverse trials in her life, Alice has learned that she is totally dependent upon God for everything, but she has a tendency to allow pride to occasionally creep into her heart when she is very tired and her focus on the Lord is redirected.

Heather: Her focus is on herself and what God can do for her. Perky and short, Heather has radiant blond hair in the latest style and penetrating green eyes that target people with circumstantial judgment during intense scrutiny of their behavior. Heather coordinates her clothes with a vibrant color scheme from head to toe to enhance a creamy and blemish-free skin type and style, matching outfits with appropriate jewelry and fashionable shoes. She is very changeable in her behavior, and her mood often depends upon the high mountains and deep valleys of life's circumstances. Heather loves hours of extensive shopping, socializing with friends, and going to movies that are reflective of society but not containing too much sex or profanity. She attempts to study the Bible, but usually something interferes to prevent any amount of significant, in-depth study, so her time in the Word is infrequent and very cursory. Heather really wants to be involved with as many ministries of the church as time permits to earn God's approval and is constantly seeking His will for her life. Heather usually has difficulty accepting God's forgiveness and love because of her sinful behavior in the past and is afraid that her life will just never measure up to God's expectations. She is constantly apologizing for some blunt and inconsiderate action and doesn't understand why God allows so many difficult situations in life if He really loves her. Often Heather worries about what Satan is doing in her life to thwart God's plan.

Their stories:

Alice: This particular day begins for Alice Buffington early in the morning with reading the Scripture, praying for her family and friends, and praising her Lord in song.

The previous day Alice was counseling a young woman named Emily who is involved in a church with focal teaching that a person is more spiritual if he does everything the pastor tells him.

Emily asked Alice if that teaching was true. Alice began explaining to Emily that God's Word was very clear that a Christian has the indwelling Holy Spirit and is led into all truth by the renewing of the mind. God has a plan for everyone, and while the pastor may direct a person to seek God's will through Bible study and prayer, counsel the believer, exhort, admonish, and correct the errors of misconception, the pastor is acting as God's servant. A pastor may offer advice that is not aligned with God's plan for an individual. God is always the final authority.

Now Alice was praying for Emily to study the Word consistently and pray for God's direction as He brought forth fruit in her life. She suggested they should pray about starting a Bible study. Initially the two of them would participate and eventually open the study to other interested people.

Heather: The day begins for Heather Cook with disorganization and lack of direction. Her three children have gotten up late and are all clamoring for her attention to help find clothes and books. The bus is arriving, and breakfast wasn't quite ready, so the children are going off to school without eating. Heather cries out to God, "Why is this happening?" and berates herself for being such a terrible mother.

After cleaning up the kitchen, Heather thinks about getting into the Word for some quiet time and direction for being a better mother, but her mind quickly redirects to the shopping trip planned later that morning with her friend Brittany. She needs a new dress to wear to her husband's office party later that week and wants to impress all his coworkers.

Heather cries out as she bangs her leg on the open dishwasher she forgot to close. Her mind goes to the constant attacks by Satan, and a spirit of fear in her heart dwells on being unable to run her home the way she should.

Observations

We observe two very different women who are walking with the Lord and reacting distinctively to their circumstances. Alice turns her focus on the Lord immediately, and Heather becomes distraught with confusion concerning her children, fear, and misdirected focus, exacerbated by the slight injury from the dishwasher. Does this mean that Alice is a better Christian than Heather? Does Alice have it together more than Heather? Can you relate to either one of these women? As you will see throughout the unpacking of this book, each believer goes through certain growth stages at a rate determined by God and His individual plan for His purpose and His glory. Alice is not without faults and shortcomings, just more spiritually mature. Heather is not hopeless and abandoned, but has great potential for spiritual growth.

Questions for Group Discussion or Individual Study

1. Compare and contrast Alice and Heather with their defined characteristics. Are they totally different? Are there any similarities?

2. Do you identify with either woman, or perhaps some characteristics of both of them? Make a list of these characteristics and think about how they relate to your relationship with the Lord.

3. What advice would you give to Alice regarding her relationship and discipleship with Emily? What would you have told Emily about her concern regarding the pastor's understanding of a person's spiritually?

4. What advice would you give to Heather regarding her relationship with God and her life as a mother? Have you experienced some of these issues with children and time management? What did you do?

5. Do you believe that God is sovereign in a believer's life? What support in the Bible do you have for either a yes or no answer? Do you have any particular examples in your life that related to God's sovereignty?

6. Why is it important to realize that Alice has a spirit of pride occasionally when her focus does not remain on the Lord? Have you ever struggled with pride regarding any experience involving your relationship with others?

7. Do you think in her earlier walk with the Lord, Alice may have experienced fears and concerns comparable to what Heather is undergoing? Since these characters are fictional, speculate what these might have been.

8. Heather seems very frazzled at this point in her life. What do you think might have an influence on her future experiences related to reactions of wisdom and calmness?

9. Why do you think Heather has difficulty with consistency for Bible study? Do you struggle with distractions when praying or studying the Bible?

10. What are some suggestions to assist in keeping your focus on the Lord and His Word? Make a list and check off each point on the list as you are able to improve your focus.

3

Don't Compare Yourself Spiritually

But Grow in grace, and in the knowledge of our Lord and Savior Jesus Christ. To him be glory both now and forever. Amen.

—2 PETER 3:18

As Christians, we have a tendency to look at other believers and form two basic comparisons. One is to elevate a perceived more spiritually mature individual, maybe in our local church or someone who is nationally known, to the level of near perfection. We look at this Christian and wonder if we will ever be as spiritually mature in our walk with the Lord. Surely this person must have special insight into God and His Word! When we look to the Scripture for answers to our dilemma, we may read in 2 Peter 1:20–21, "Knowing this first that no prophecy of the scripture is of any private interpretation. For the prophecy came not in old time by the will of man: but holy men of God spake as they were moved by the Holy Ghost." Everyone is exposed to the same truth in God's Word, but the individual maturity level in a Christian's spiritual life determines the depth of biblical understanding. Colossians 1:9 expounds upon this truth of spiritual growth as the apostle Paul encourages the maturing believer: "For this cause we also, since the day we heard it, do not cease to pray for you, and to desire that ye might be filled with the knowledge of his will in all wisdom and spiritual understanding." As we grow in Christ, our wisdom and knowledge expand exponentially at the rate determined by God for His purpose and glory. With this understanding we are able to trust in the Lord's direction and not our own efforts, which are often found to be ineffectual in accomplishment or detrimental to our life's purpose.

Another common comparison made by Christians is the perception of other Christians not knowing as much truth or having as much wisdom and maturity as we do. If the rate of growth is rapid for a new believer, the temptation may be to become proud in the knowledge that is imparted to the young Christian by the Lord. Along with this increased wisdom and understanding, the believer will be transformed through trials and experiences resulting in bearing the fruit of self-control and gentleness to temper the response to the quick growth spurt. Colossians 1:10 will support this concept: "That ye might walk worthy of the Lord unto all pleasing, being fruitful in every good work, and increasing in the knowledge of God." Walking with the Lord moment by moment is the most wonderful life a person can experience. Unbelievers may assume that being a Christian is dull and boring; why would someone want to give up having a good time to follow a set of rules and not experience all the pleasures of the world? The answer to that question is, of course, that life as a Christian is what God has enabled us to experience by sending His only Son to die on the cross for our sins so we may be reconciled to a relationship with the Lord for eternity. We are now free, not to indulge in behavior that the Bible proclaims to be sinful, but to serve the Lord in the ministry to which we have been called as we have been liberated from the bondage of sin. We see this truth very transparently in 2 Corinthians 3:17: "Now the Lord is that Spirit: And where the Spirit of the Lord is, there is liberty."

God never intended for us to compare ourselves to or compete with other believers, but to keep our eyes focused on Him and His Word. The only comparison we should contemplate is between ourselves and the Lord Jesus Christ, a comparison where we always fall short. Romans 3:23 states, "For all have sinned, and come short of the glory of God." God does not, however, leave an unbeliever without a divine answer to have an eternal relationship with Him. Romans 3:24 postulates, "Being justified freely by his grace through the redemption that is in Christ Jesus." Once we belong to the Lord Jesus Christ, there is no longer any wrath or condemnation levied from God to the believer for eternity. This truth is supported in Romans 8:1: "There is therefore now no condemnation to them which are in Christ Jesus, who walk not after the flesh, but after the Spirit."

As we consider Alice and Heather, a natural conclusion based upon the information in chapter 2 might be that Alice is very mature and able to serve the Lord without any difficulty, while Heather is very immature and unable to accomplish much for the Lord. A mental illustration might be to visualize Alice perched on top of a pedestal and Heather on hands and knees groping around on the floor for answers to her problems.

The realistic answer is that Alice and Heather are exactly at the spiritual growth level that God has ordained individually for them at this point in time.

If you are a believer in the Lord Jesus Christ, you are also walking in grace at the spiritual growth level where God has you. We will consider four stages of Christian growth as delineated in the Bible and examine each stage in chapter 5, enabling us to scrutinize the truth about spiritual maturity.

Questions for Group Discussion or Individual Study

1. Have you ever compared yourself to another Christian? What was the particular reason for the comparison? How did that make you feel toward the other believer?

2. When you read chapter 2, did you think that Alice was a "better Christian" than Heather? Why or why not? What constitutes the level of maturity according to what you believe the Bible teaches?

3. Have you ever placed another believer on a pedestal? Why did you do that? How did that make you feel? Did you later change your mind about the person you elevated in your thinking? What circumstance caused the change, and how did that relate to your understanding of the Bible?

4. Have you ever thought you were "not as spiritual" as another believer who seems to react correctly during life's difficult situations? Did that make you feel that you didn't have enough faith or that you were a failure? Does the Bible substantiate that type of thinking? Provide Scriptures for your answer.

5. What Scripture verses can you think of that would support the individuality of a believer? Are there any Scriptures that teach that all Christians will be alike or pursue the same ministries? Support your answer to this question.

6. Do you think God loves a mature believer more than a fairly young Christian? Why or why not? Support your answers with Scripture.

7. Have you ever looked at your life and compared it to the life that Jesus Christ lived when He walked this earth? How did you feel about your life when you made the comparison? Can you ever be without sin as He was when He walked this earth?

8. Do you think that God wants you to feel guilty for your sin? Why or why not? Defend your answer from Scripture. What is Christian liberty compared to the bondage of an unbeliever?

9. What do you believe the death of Jesus Christ on the cross accomplished? Have you ever really thought about the purpose for the cross

and what it means to you personally? Do you ever see yourself at the foot of the cross looking up? How does that make you feel?

10. Why do you think that Alice and Heather might be at different stages in their spiritual growth? Does going to church, teaching Sunday school, or serving in the community give you more credibility with God?

4

When Does Christian Growth Begin?

And he shall be like a tree planted by the rivers of water, that bringeth forth his fruit in his season; his leaf also shall not wither; and whatsoever he doeth shall prosper.

—Psalm 1:3

When we are contemplating the onset of Christian growth, Psalm 1:3 provides an appropriate simile comparing the growth of a believer to that of a tree with roots planted deeply by the nourishing water that produces abundant fruit in the correct season. This chapter will explore the comparison between a Christian and a tree to elucidate the understanding of Christian growth.

Growth of a Tree

In order for the life of a tree to begin, a seed must be planted in the ground. Whether through natural sprouting by germination from another tree or seeds sown in the fall that germinate the following spring, a tree will begin to grow.

The actual process of growth occurs as the tree produces new cells in a limited number of places; cell division transpires in these places called meristems, zones of intense activity where new cells are formed and expanded. Meristems located at the branch tips affect the growth in height of a tree. The roots of the tree expand through the soil due to the apical meristems facilitating tip growth. Apical meristems are also situated in the buds formed on the tree, while a meristem called vascular cambium affects the growth of the trunk diameter.[1]

We enjoy beholding the fruit of a tree, whether it is plucking a red, ripe, luscious apple, experiencing the delicious fragrance of honeysuckle, or savoring the blossoms of an azalea that are very pleasing to the eye.

The rate of growth of fruit on the tree depends upon the richness of the soil, the abundance of sunshine, and the absorption of sufficient amounts of water by the roots of the tree. If these components are neglected, the tree will produce an inferior quality of fruit, or even fail to thrive.

Growth of a Christian

We can compare Christian growth to the growth of a tree. The planting of the seed of a tree correlates with the union we have in Christ upon salvation: Ephesians 1:13: "In whom ye also trusted after that ye heard the word of truth, the gospel of your salvation: in whom also after that ye believed ye were sealed with that holy spirit of promise."

Next, we have growth below the ground that cannot be seen by the human eye as the tree's root system migrates through the soil. Compare this growth of tree roots to the Christian who is being renewed by the Word of God internally. The renewal of the believer begins immediately upon salvation, with external evidence appearing over time while continuous growth is occurring. Colossians 1:3–6 states, "We give thanks to God and the Father of our Lord Jesus Christ, praying always for you. Since we heard of your faith in Christ Jesus, and of the love which ye have to all the saints. For the hope which is laid up for you in heaven, whereof ye heard before in the word of the truth of the gospel. Which is come unto you, as it is in all the world; and *bringeth forth fruit*, as it doth also in you, *since the day ye heard of it and know the grace of God in truth.*" The renewal of the Christian is entirely the work of the Holy Spirit, as seen in 2 Corinthians 3:18, "But we all with open face beholding as in a glass the glory of the Lord, *are changed* into the same image from glory to glory, even as by the Spirit of the Lord" as demonstrated grammatically by the passive verb "are changed," indicating the growth is being done to the believer, not from any effort exerted by the believer.

When the tree begins to have visible growth above the ground and the Christian's transformed life becomes apparent, a comparison can be inferred. Romans 12:2 expounds this concept: "and be not conformed to this world: but be ye transformed by the renewing of your mind, that ye may prove what is that good, and acceptable, and perfect will of God." We received the Lord Jesus Christ by faith as a gift from God, not from anything we have done. "For by grace are ye saved through faith: and that not of yourselves: it is the gift of God. Not of works, lest any man should boast" (Eph. 2:8–9). Our continuous transforming walk will demonstrate this outpouring of faith. "As ye have therefore received Christ Jesus the Lord, *so walk ye in him*: rooted and built up in him and stablished in the faith as ye have been taught, abounding therein with thanksgiving" (Col. 2:6–7). We received the Lord Jesus Christ by faith, and we walk the same way, not by exercising our will, but by our ongoing total transformation by the Holy Spirit.

Just as there is a variance of growth rate in the budding and blooming of a tree, the fruit of the believer is manifested over time in various degrees of abundance. "But the fruit of the spirit is love, joy, peace, long-suffering, gentleness, goodness, faith, meekness, temperance" (Gal. 5:22–23). Just as the fruit on a tree may be at different stages of maturity, the believer's fruit will be more prolific in some areas and just beginning to bud in others. Joy may be very apparent in the exuberance of a believer, but patience with other people may be sparse. The trials God brings into a Christian's life will determine the particular fruit that is being renewed to bring glory to the Lord. "That we might walk worthy of the Lord unto all pleasing, being fruitful in every good work, and increasing in the knowledge of God; Strengthened with all might, according to his glorious power, unto all patience and long-suffering with joyfulness" (Col. 1:10–11). As the roots of the tree are secured in the ground, allowing the tree to withstand the vicious elements of the weather, the Christian stands firm in the truth of God's Word through continuous renewal of the mind. "That we henceforth be no more children, tossed to and fro, and carried about with every wind of doctrine by the sleight of men, and cunning craftiness, whereby they lie in wait to deceive" (Eph. 4:14).

When each of these components is merged, the following illustration shows the complete overall picture of Christian growth.

This illustration, which will be unpacked in the next chapter when the growth stages of a Christian are examined in greater detail, depicts a tree and its roots; the illustration contains all of the stages of growth from our union with the Lord Jesus Christ to the development of the fruit of the Spirit in our lives. Without the depth of our Christian roots in the Word of God with its rich doctrinal truth, we may resemble the Lord on the outside, but inside we have no depth of the Lord's true character. Have you ever taken a red and de-licious-looking apple, bitten into the appealing skin, and discovered brown

rottenness? That is similar to the person who talks about being a Christian but is only acting out the tenets of the law and not walking in the liberty of Jesus Christ. "Now the Lord is that Spirit: and where the Spirit of the Lord is, there is liberty" (2 Cor. 3:17).

The rate of growth of a believer in Jesus Christ depends upon several factors in a Christian's life. These parameters include the richness of the truth in God's Word, the abundance of the believer's immersion into the Word, and the absorption of sufficient amounts of beholding God's truth through spiritual understanding. Each of these factors occurs at a rate predetermined by God in the life of each believer for the purpose of God's glory. Unlike a tree that will fail to thrive without the richness of the soil, the abundance of sunshine, and the absorption of sufficient amounts of water through its roots, a person who is genuinely rooted and grounded in Christ will continue to grow. This forward growth occurs as the Christian continuously feeds on the Word of God for spiritual nourishment and walks in its truth at a predetermined rate and in the particular areas of focus and study according to God's ordained plan for each individual believer. Ephesians 2:10 states, "For we are his workmanship created in Christ Jesus unto good works, which God hath before ordained that we should walk in them." This growth of a believer in no way assumes perfection, but allows for growth spurts as well as times of wandering that may be construed as a lack of growth. The Lord brings trials into our lives to demonstrate His work of grace as we grow through times of losing our focus on the truth of God's plan and walking in sin or rebellion. Our response to these trials may range from fear and trepidation to trusting God for the outcome of maturing us in the faith. Scriptures that help us see this spectrum are Psalm 91:5–6, "Thou shalt not be afraid for the terror by night; nor for the arrow that flieth by day; Nor for the pestilence that walketh in darkness; nor for the destruction that wasteth at noonday," and Romans 5:3–5, "And not only so but we glory in tribulations also: knowing that tribulation worketh patience; And patience, experience; and experience, hope: And hope maketh not ashamed; because the love of God is shed abroad in our hearts by the Holy Ghost which is given unto us." The faithfulness of the Lord will bring us back in alignment with His truth as He uses circumstances, people, and our own misconceptions to behold His truth.

Sanctification

Now let's look a little deeper and examine the process of sanctification as taught in the Word of God, to tie together the concepts of the growth of a believer to the entire relationship we have with God from the calling and wooing of His elect until their final destination of heaven.

Sanctification can be defined as the setting apart of the believer before and during salvation. There are four components of sanctification:

- prejustification sanctification
- justifying sanctification
- progressive sanctification
- ultimate sanctification

Refer to chart 2 in the appendix: "Sanctification." We need to examine each component with supporting Scriptures to validate and to clarify our growth pattern as believers.

Prejustification Sanctification

Focusing on prejustification sanctification initially, as you can see from the outline, an important scripture to examine for clarification is 2 Thessalonians 2:13–14: "But we are bound to give thanks always to God for you, brethren beloved of the Lord, because God hath from the beginning chosen you to salvation through sanctification of the Spirit and belief of the truth. Whereunto he called you by our gospel, to the obtaining of the glory of our Lord Jesus Christ."

The Holy Spirit's work in prejustification sanctification is to protect God's elect until salvation, bring the elect under the hearing of the gospel, open up the understanding of the elect, and to give the gift of faith through the hearing of the Word.

Protection of God's Elect until Salvation

We will now explore the time involved from an individual's biological birth until the moment of salvation, concerning the protection of God's elect by the Holy Spirit. Have you ever wondered why some people die in a vehicle crash, while others walk away unscathed? Or have you ever had a near-death experience resulting from a medical emergency? It was probably very frightening and perhaps caused you to consider your spiritual destiny. Since the work of the Holy Spirit is to bring the believer to God, escaping these potential death experiences is probably related to this protection by the Holy Spirit.

Bringing the Elect under the Hearing of the Gospel

Some people seem to be interested in spiritual things and may appear to be seeking after God, but Romans 3:11 states, "THERE IS NONE THAT UNDERSTANDITH, THERE IS NONE THAT SEEKETH AFTER GOD." This is a quote from Psalms 10:7 of the Old Testament. In John 6:44 we have more clarification of God's calling: "No man can come to me, except the Father which hast sent me draw him; and I will raise him up at the last day." And in John 6:37 we read, "All that the Father giveth me shall come to me: and him that cometh to me I will in no wise cast out." When you read Ephesians 2:1, "and you hath he quickened who were dead in trespasses and sins," the conclusion is that a dead person seeks after no one. Can a dead man do anything for himself? The obvious answer is no. Neither can a spiritually dead person do anything until his faith in the Lord Jesus Christ makes him alive spiritually. This truth is illustrated clearly in Romans 5:21: "That as sin hath reigned unto death, even so might grace reign through righteousness unto eternal life by Jesus Christ our Lord."

Do we exercise our own will in life? Salvation is compared to creation in 2 Corinthians 4:6: "For God who commanded the light to shine out of darkness, hath shined in our hearts, to give the light of the knowledge of the glory of God in the face of Jesus Christ." Could darkness create light? We hear a resounding no! The Holy Spirit was necessary to bring the light of salvation. In John 1:4 ("in him was life; and the life was the light of men"), Jesus Christ is called light. John 1:11–13 shows us that salvation is an act of God not of man's capability: "He came unto his own, and his own received him not. But as many as received him, to them gave he power to become the sons of God, even to them that believe on his name: which were born, not of blood, nor of the will of the flesh, nor of the will of man, but of God." We have been brought to and enlightened by God to receive the Holy Spirit.

In 1 Corinthians 2:12–14 we read, "Now we have received, not the spirit of the world, but the spirit which is of God: that we might know the things that are freely given to us of God. Which things also we speak, not in the word which man's wisdom teacheth, but which the Holy Ghost teacheth; But the natural man receiveth not the things of the Spirit of God: for they are foolishness unto him: neither can he know them, because they are spiritually discerned." These Scriptures support that we have to hear the gospel to be saved. The Holy Spirit is the one who is preparing our heart to receive the spiritual truth before we are even able to understand its essence, since the unsaved individual cannot understand spiritual truth, which is foolishness to him.

Opening up the Understanding of the Elect

In John 12:40, a passage from Isaiah 6:9 is quoted as saying "HE HATH BLINDED THEIR EYES, AND HARDENED THEIR HEART, THAT THEY SHOULD NOT SEE WITH THEIR EYES, NOR UNDERSTAND

WITH THEIR HEART, AND BE CONVERTED, AND I SHOULD HEAL THEM." To further expound upon opening up the eyes of understanding of the elect, we read in Ephesians 1:17–18, "That the God of our Lord Jesus Christ, the Father of glory, may give unto you the spirits of wisdom and revelation in the knowledge of him: the eyes of your understanding being enlightened: that ye may know what is the hope of his calling, and what the riches of the glory of his inheritance in the saints." We must, therefore, be exposed to the gospel with our ears and/or eyes and understand with our hearts and believe. Perhaps you were exposed to the gospel several times before you actually heard it. God's appointed time for the eyes of your understanding being enlightened has already been determined and will not be hastened or thwarted by anyone or any circumstance.

Giving the Gift of Faith through the Hearing of the Word

When studying Ephesians 2: 8–9 ("For by grace are ye saved through faith: and that not of yourselves: it is the gift of God: not of works, lest any man should boast") and Romans 10:17 ("So then faith comes by hearing, and hearing by the word of God"), the conclusion may be reached that faith is a gift from God, not of an act of the will of man.

Justifying Sanctification

Next, justifying sanctification, also known as positional sanctification, is supported by Acts 26:18: "to open their eyes and to turn them from darkness to light, and from the power of Satan unto God, that they may receive forgiveness of sins, and inheritance among them which are sanctified by faith that is in me." This refers to the setting apart of the believer into the Body of Christ at *the time* they trust the Lord Jesus Christ as Savior.

The definition of "sanctify" and the grammatical usage as delineated by Zodhiates is as follows: "Sanctify (*hagiazo*)(hag-ee-ad-zo) PFPP (perfect participle passive-stresses the *state* (permanent) brought about by the finished results of the action. The subject receives the action of the verb. This means that the person is brought into this permanent state." Sanctification is that relationship with God into which men enter by faith in Christ: "Therefore, being justified by faith, we have peace with God through our Lord Jesus Christ: by whom also we have access by faith into this grace wherein we stand, and rejoice in hope of the glory of God" (Rom. 5:1–2).

In the process of justifying sanctification, a person goes from the state of being in Adam to being in Christ, or from darkness to light. "Giving thanks unto the Father, which hath made us meet to be partakers of the inheritance of the saints in light: Who hath delivered us from the power of darkness, and hath translated us into the kingdom of his dear Son" is found in Colossians 1:12–13. Genesis 1:27 states that man was created in the image of God. Genesis 3 describes how Adam fell into sin through disobedience. This condition of man's fallen state is what we refer to as the "sin nature." We are all born with it and are essentially in Adam. In chart 3 in the appendix ("Old Man/New Man"), the black circle above Old Man indicates our union with Adam and that our spirit is dead. Romans 5:12 states, "Wherefore, as by one man sin entered into the world, and death by sin; and so death passed upon all men, for that all have sinned." The one man referred to in this verse is Adam. We have a dead spirit and will have a mind to sin and continue in this sin until we physically die. In Romans 3:23 we read, " For all have sinned and come short of the glory of God" and in Romans 6:23a, "For the wages of sin is death." The plus sign above New Man represents our union with the Lord Jesus Christ and the indwelling Holy Spirit. Looking in 2 Corinthians 5:17, we see that we have passed from death to life as a "new creation." This means we are an entirely new creature. Our minds are renewed by the leading of the Holy Spirit into all truth in the word of God and we bear fruit. Romans 12:2 clearly reads, "And be not conformed to this world: but be ye transformed by the renewing of your mind, that ye may prove what is that good, and acceptable, and perfect will of God." It is impossible to be in union with Adam and in union with Christ at the same time. Romans 6:6 elucidates this truth: "Knowing this, that our old man is crucified with him, that the body of sin might be destroyed, that henceforth we should not serve sin." The Greek word used in this verse is *katargeo*, which is defined as "abolish, cease, or destroy." When Paul uses this word in his epistles, it is rendered a complete, not temporary or partial ceasing. And Romans 6:13 states, "Neither yield ye your members as instruments of unrighteousness unto sin: but yield yourselves unto God, as those that are alive from the dead, and your members as instruments of righteousness unto God." Also in Romans 9:23 we read, "And that he might make known the riches of his glory on the vessels of mercy, which he had afore prepared unto glory." Our choices, therefore, are made from a renewed mind, not exercising our will.

In the Old Testament, righteousness was pursued by attempting to keep the law. When the law was broken, a sacrifice was made in the temple. This sacrifice never justified the transgressor; it just provided a covering until the coming of the promised Messiah. To understand this concept, we read in Galatians 3:22–25, "But the Scripture hath concluded all under sin, that the promise by faith of Jesus Christ might be given to them that believe. But before faith came, we were kept under the law, shut up unto the faith which should afterwards be revealed. Wherefore the law was our schoolmaster to bring us unto Christ, that we might be justified by faith. But after that faith is come, we are no longer under a schoolmaster. For ye are all the children of God by faith in Christ Jesus." In 1 Corinthians 1:30, we see that we are in Christ and He is our righteousness: "But of him are ye in Christ Jesus, who of God is made unto us wisdom, and righteousness, and sanctification, and redemption." Also in John 1:17, the contrast between law and grace is very clear: "For the law was given by Moses, but grace and truth came by Jesus Christ." In 2 Corinthians 5:21, we see that we are righteous by Christ through justification: "For he hath made him to be sin offering for us, who knew no sin; that we might be made the righteousness of God in him." So, sanctification is being set apart into Christ, and justification is the result of our faith in Christ.

Hebrews 10:10–14 shows believers to be sanctified once and for all by the offering of Christ: "10. By the which will we are sanctified through the offering of the body of Jesus Christ, once for all. 11. And every priest standeth daily ministering and offering oftentimes the same sacrifices, which can never take away sins: 12. But this man, after he had offered one sacrifice for sins for ever, sat down on the right hand of God: 13. From henceforth expecting till his enemies be made his footstool. 14. For by one offering he hath perfected for ever them that are sanctified." We see a contrast between the Old Testament and the New Testament in verses 11 and 12 respectively. In verse 14 we see that we are perfected forever.

Two verses in Romans demonstrate that it was Abraham's belief in God that was put to his account for righteousness and justification: "For what saith the Scripture? Abraham believed God, and it was counted unto him for righteousness" (4:3) and "And therefore it was imputed to him for righteousness" (4:22).

The Body of Christ is shown to be sanctified in Acts 20:32, "And now, brethren, I commend you to God, and to the word of his grace, which is able to build you up, and to give you and inheritance among all them which are sanctified," and in Romans 15:16, "That I should be the minister of Jesus Christ to the Gentiles, ministering the gospel of God that the offering up of the Gentiles might be acceptable, being sanctified by the Holy Ghost."

Progressive Sanctification

The third component of sanctification is supported by Romans 8:28–29, "And we know that all things work together for good to them that love God, to them who are the called according to his purpose. For whom he did foreknow, he also did *predestinate to be conformed to the image of his son*, that he might be the first-born among many brethren," and John 17:17, "Sanctify them through thy truth: thy word is truth."

The Believer Is Set Apart by God for a Purpose

In Romans 8:29, the Greek word "foreknow" or *proginosko* is in the aorist indicative active (AINA) tense, which refers to a verb related to one point in time, accomplished by the subject. The subject in this Scripture, of course, is God. The definition of "foreknow" is "to perceive or recognize beforehand, to know previously." In this Scripture *proginosko* appears with the verb *proorise*, which means "did predestinate."

"Predestinate" also means "to determine or decree a purpose beforehand." Two other Scriptures using *proginosko* in this same context are Ephesians 1:5, "Having predestinated us unto the adoption of children by Jesus Christ to himself, according to the good pleasure of his will," and Ephesians 1:11, "In whom also we have obtained an inheritance, being predestinated according to the purpose of him who worketh all things after the counsel of his own will."

This foreknowledge and foreordination in the Scripture is always unto salvation and not unto perdition. The word "knowing" here denotes a previous uniting of oneself with someone. The salvation of every believer is known and determined in the mind of God before its actual accomplishment in an historical setting. *Proginosko*, "to foreknow," corresponds with having been chosen before the foundation of the world, "According as he hath chosen us in him before the foundation of the world, that we should be holy and without blame before him in love" (Eph. 1:4). God has always foreknown us or been in union with us, even though we didn't know Him as the elect.

In Amos 3:2 in the Old Testament, "You only have I known of all the families of the earth: therefore I will punish you for all your iniquities," the Hebrew word for "known" is *yada*, meaning "to know, ascertain by seeing, setting the heart upon." This refers to Israel being foreknown.

Acts 2:23 states, "Him, being delivered by the determinate counsel and foreknowledge of God, ye have taken, and by wicked hands have crucified and slain." The Greek word "foreknowledge" is *prognosis*, which denotes "the foreordained relation of the fellowship of God with the objects of His saving counsel." Foreknowledge also involves "a resolution formed beforehand." Within the Scripture the Greek word *kai* translated as "and" means a "cumulative force." One word is a further description of the other. So, we would have the death, burial, and resurrection being foreknown.

In Romans 8:29 the word "predestinate" is often confused with the doctrine of election. *Election means a choice of people.* God chooses some who will put their faith in the Lord Jesus Chris and have salvation. *Predestination means a choice of purpose.* There is no element of choice of people, but of purpose. The word means to set a boundary or limit in advance. The purpose in this Scripture is that we will be conformed to the image of His Son. This is where the character of the Lord Jesus Christ is worked out by the renewing of our mind. As believers, we are set apart and protected by God as if we have a fence around us. Nothing can penetrate the fence unless it is for our benefit to be conformed to Christ. When Satan throws his fiery darts, they can be quenched as they project over the fence. Satan cannot, however, enter through the fence. This truth is clarified in Job 1:8–12:

> And the Lord said unto Satan, Hath thou considered my servant Job, that there is none like him on the earth, a perfect and an upright man, one that feareth God, and escheweth evil? Then Satan answered the Lord, and said, Doth Job fear God for nought? Hast not thou made a hedge about him, and about his house, and about all that he hath on every side? Thou hast blessed the work of his hands, and his substance is increased in the land. But put forth thine hand now, and touch all that he hath, and he will curse thee to thy face. And the Lord said unto Satan, Behold all that he hath is in thy power; only upon himself put not forth thy hand. So Satan went forth from the presence of the Lord.

When Satan questioned the hedge of prosperity and health God had placed around Job, God allowed him to inflict whatever he chose upon Job except death. As Job suffered much and refused to curse God, everything was restored to him in abundance: "And the Lord turned the captivity of Job, when he prayed for his friends: also the Lord gave Job twice as much as he had before" (Job 42:10). God always redeems the time for His elect: "Walk in wisdom toward them that are without, redeeming the time" (Col. 4:5).

In Romans 8:29 the Greek word *summorphos* means "formed together with." The context of meaning in this verse is the conforming of children of God to the image of His son. In Philippians 3:21, "Who shall change our vile body, that it may be fashioned like unto his glorious body, according to the working whereby he is able even to subdue all things unto himself," "fashioned like unto," or *summorphos*, refers to a conforming to His body of glory. There are two types of conforming. One is the outward conformity against the inward nature. This is like a masquerade where the true identity of the person is concealed. In Romans 12:2 "conformed," which is the Greek word *suschematizo*, means "no inward transformation." The present imperative active (PIM) tense is used for this verb, which only occurs in the active and middle voices in the New Testament. The active voice may indicate a command to do something in the future that involves continuous or repeated action. The other type of conforming in Romans 8:29 means that the inward nature takes an outward transformation, one having the same form as the other.

The Believer Is Set Apart by the Word of God

John 17:17, "Sanctify them through thy truth: thy word is truth," uses the Greek word *hagiazo* for "sanctify." The tense used is aorist imperative active (AIMA), which denotes command, request, or entreaty; action is being accomplished by the subject of the verb. This tense does not involve a command for continuous or repetitive action. Instead, it is often used for general exhortations and for things that must begin at that very moment. The separation of the believer from the world in his behavior is by the Father through the Word.

Acts 20:32, "And now, brethren, I commend you to God, and to the word of his grace, which is able to build you up, and to give you an inheritance among all them which are sanctified," and Romans 15:16, "That I should be the minister of Jesus Christ to the Gentiles, ministering the gospel of God, that the offering up of the Gentiles might be acceptable, being sanctified by the Holy Ghost," are other examples of the setting apart of the believer for God.

Another example of being set apart for God is in John 10:36, "Say ye of him, whom the Father hath sanctified, and sent into the world, thou blasphemest because I said, I am the Son of God," which shows us that God the Father set Jesus apart from the Godhead to die on the cross.

Chapter 5 will unpack the specifics of growing in Christ during the time period of progressive sanctification.

Ultimate Sanctification

The fourth and final component of sanctification occurs when the believer is completely set apart in heaven. Philippians 3:20–21 portrays the glory of that much-anticipated day: "For our conversation is in heaven; from whence also we look for the Savior, the Lord Jesus Christ: Who shall change our vile body, that it may be fashioned like unto his glorious body, according to the working whereby he is able even to subdue all things unto himself." The ultimate state of the believer is the transition from progressive sanctification to ultimate sanctification, often referred to as glorification, when the Christian arrives in heaven to live with the Lord Jesus Christ for eternity.

Questions for Group Discussion or Individual Study

1. Compare the growth of a tree to the growth of a Christian. What are the basic similarities? What are the basic differences?

2. Discuss the process of growth beginning with the initial planting of the seed. Use the Scriptures given and cross-reference other Scriptures from your own study.

3. Examine the illustration of the tree bearing fruit to synthesize the process of our union with Christ as a believer related to the actual spiritual growth occurring as we grow at different rates. Read the Scriptures in the text and discuss their relevance to the process.

4. What is the definition of sanctification? Use your concordance to identify Scriptures in the Bible where this word is used and discuss the application to the Body of Christ.

5. Name the four components of sanctification. Discuss each one and provide supporting Scriptures.

6. Have you ever had an experience when you thought you were going to die? Did you ever feel that someone was watching out for you? How do you explain either one of these? Why does God let some people die and others live during plane crashes, car crashes, or a war?

7. Do you remember the moment when the Lord Jesus Christ became your Savior? Do you think you chose that moment? What does the phrase "old man" mean? Is this different or the same as being a new creature? Support your answer with Scripture.

8. Are the terms "election" and "predestination" synonymous? How are they alike? How are they different? Do you believe that you direct your own life by choices you make? Where does God fit into all of this?

9. Do you ever think about what heaven is like? We do not have many Scriptures that describe heaven in detail. Do you think those who have gone to heaven are able to see what we are doing here? Who do you think you will see when you get there? Do you believe that you are definitely going to heaven? Why or why not?

10. Think about your personal relationship with the Lord and how each component of sanctification applies to your spiritual life.

5

The Four Stages Related to Christian Growth

For the hope which is laid up for you in heaven, whereof ye heard before in the word of the truth of the gospel; which is come unto you, as it is in all the world; and bringeth forth fruit, as it doth also in you, since the day ye heard of it, and knew the grace of God in truth.

—COLOSSIANS 1:5–6

Chart 4 in the appendix, "Growth Stages of a Christian," shows the four specific stages a believer will grow through from salvation to the end of his physical life on earth. Each stage is supported by Scriptures, but there are several cross-references that are relevant to the spiritual transformation that occurs in a believer during the progressive sanctification process. You are encouraged to use a concordance to locate the cross-references as you further your study of God's Word in the area of spiritual transformation. The definition and expansion of progressive sanctification can be found in chapter 4. Each of the four stages will be examined closely, and Alice Buffington and Heather Cook, described in detail in chapter 2, will be used as examples to clarify where they fit into the hierarchy of Christian growth.

Growth Stages of a Christian
Newborn Babes

The first stage of growth the new believer enters into is the newborn babe. 1 Peter 2:2 states, "As newborn babes, desire the sincere milk of the word, that ye may grow thereby." The spiritual characteristics of this initial growth stage are that newborn babes desire the sincere milk of the Word to grow, they want to eat, they grow rapidly, they can't feed themselves, and they need a mother to bring things close because they can't see too far. We will examine each of these spiritual characteristics closely to garner more understanding of their relationship to the growth of a believer. The spiritual characteristics will also be compared to the growth of a human being in a parallel fashion.

Newborn Babes Desire the Sincere Milk of the Word to Grow

When a person places his faith in the Lord Jesus Christ as Savior, he becomes a new creature in Christ. At this juncture, he may be compared to a baby that has just been born. Many mothers choose to breastfeed their baby, which has been shown to provide the following benefits:

1. A healthier baby. "The incidences of pneumonia, colds and viruses are reduced among breastfed babies," according to infant-nutrition expert Ruth A. Lawrence, MD, a professor of pediatrics and OB-GYN at the University of Rochester School of Medicine and Dentistry in Rochester, New York.

2. Long-term protection. Breastfeeding reduces the baby's risk of developing chronic conditions such as type I diabetes, celiac disease and Crohn's disease.

3. Lower risk of sudden infant death syndrome. Breastfeeding lowers your baby's risk of sudden infant death syndrome, or SIDS, by about half.

4. Less risk of cancer. Breastfeeding can decrease a baby's risk of some childhood cancers.

5. A custom-made supply. Formula isn't able to change its constitution, but breast milk morphs to meet a baby's changing needs. Colostrum production begins during pregnancy and continues through the early days of breastfeeding. Colostrum is extremely easy to digest and is therefore the perfect first food for baby. It is low in volume (measurable in teaspoons rather than ounces) but high in concentrated nutrition for the newborn. The concentration of immune factors is much higher in colostrum than in mature milk and works as a natural and 100 percent safe vaccine, containing large quantities of an antibody called secretory immunoglobulin A (IgA), which is a new substance to the newborn. Colostrum also contains high concentrations of leukocytes, protective white cells that can destroy disease-causing bacteria and viruses. The colostrum gradually changes to mature milk during the first two weeks after birth; the concentrations of the antibodies in the milk decrease, but the milk volume greatly increases. The disease-fighting properties

of human milk do not disappear with the colostrum, but as long as the baby receives breast milk, he or she will receive immunological protection against many different viruses and bacteria.[1]

Often breastfeeding does not work out due to medical complications or the desire of the mother, and the baby will be fed with a bottle. The importance of the baby having pure milk without chemicals or preservatives is apparent for proper growth and nutrition. Either method of feeding will result in the growth of the baby.

Similarly, the baby Christian needs the pure "milk" of the Word, which is the truth at a level that will be spiritually understood. One of the names of God, El Shaddai, means "the all sufficient one."[2] The Hebrew word *shad* or *shadayim*, meaning "the breast," occurs twenty-four times as *Shaddai*. This particular meaning is "one who nourishes, supplies, and satisfies." Isaiah 66:10–13 states,

> Rejoice ye with Jerusalem, and be glad with her, all ye that love her; rejoice for joy with her, all ye that mourn for her: That ye may suck and be satisfied with the breasts of her consolations; that ye may milk out, and be delighted with the abundance of her glory. For thus saith the Lord, Behold, I will extend peace to her like a river, and the glory of the Gentiles like a flowing stream: then shall ye suck, ye shall be borne upon her sides, and be dandled upon her knees. As one whom his mother comforteth, so will I comfort you; and ye shall be comforted in Jerusalem.

This meaning of *Shaddai* as "the breast" applied to the word for God, *El*, now means "one mighty to nourish, satisfy, and supply." The comparison of the baby Christian to the human baby now becomes very clear and precious. When a new Christian is exposed to the Word of God that is accurate and correctly interpreted, he will discern what God has for him at that particular level of his growth. When the same area of Scripture is taught in later years, the wisdom and knowledge that is beheld at that time will be discerned at the higher level of growth the person has attained. We cannot expect a baby to get up and out of the crib simply because we say, "Get up and walk across the room." His body, although possessing the essential neurological equipment at birth, must mature over time as the baby progresses from arm and leg movements to rolling, crawling, kneeling, standing, and ultimately walking. Likewise, as a teacher of the Word, one cannot expect a babe in Christ to walk in the truth he has not yet grown into through the renewal of his mind. We can concur, therefore, that a person is at the level of spiritual growth God has ordained at any given point in time.

Newborn Babes Want to Eat

The crucial thing a baby desires, besides having a loving touch and staying dry, is to eat. Talk to any mother of a newborn, and you will hear the stories of babies eating every two hours, and once satisfied with a full tummy, going to sleep. That routine is constantly repeated day and night, and the baby often never appears to run out of the desire to eat. A baby will cry when hungry and will not be satisfied until he has eaten the amount he desires. What a joy to watch a baby that is full of milk only to have that one small drop of milk slowly slide from the mouth to his chin as his eyes look adoringly into the contented eyes of his mother.

Similarly, a newborn believer usually has a strong desire to be exposed to the truth of God's Word and will be often found talking to anyone who will listen to a plethora of questions. The newly discovered excitement of a person who has been recently ushered into the Body of Christ is often contagious to a more mature believer. The Word of God and its truth becomes like very enticing spiritual food, and the new believer's appetite is difficult to satiate. Many of the questions posed to those who will listen may appear very basic, such as "Who wrote the Bible?" or more challenging, such as "Can you explain the Trinity to me?" Each newly discovered truth in God's Word becomes another rare jewel to be extracted and admired for its worth; the wonderment of beholding truth will renew the baby believer's mind as he advances down the spiritual road of being conformed to the image of the Lord Jesus Christ.

Newborn Babies Grow Rapidly

As the newborn baby continues to eat, he will grow very quickly during the first year of life. According to Dr. Jay L. Hoecker, a pediatrician in

Rochester, Minnesota, who sees patients at the Mayo Clinic, "Healthy infants come in a range of sizes. Still infant growth tends to follow a fairly predictable path." [3]

There are certain guidelines to consider for infant growth during the first year of life: A baby should double the birth weight by about five months and triple the birth weight when reaching one year of age. Sometimes healthy babies go through brief periods when they stop gaining weight or even lose some weight. Since a pediatrician usually charts the baby's weight at each visit, the individual baby's position on the curve of the growth chart is not as crucial as the trend of the overall curve.

When a newborn Christian hungers for truth from the Word of God, he consumes the spiritual food while sitting under the instruction of a teacher in a Bible study or a pastor at church, and often grows very rapidly in his basic understanding of the Scriptures as applied to his life.

Newborn Babies Can't Feed Themselves

The human baby is totally dependent upon another person for nourishment and is unable to acquire food when hungry. Whether the mother nurses the child or feeds the baby with a bottle, independence is not available for eating at this stage of human growth. The baby is very faithful to inform his family when hungry by exercising his lung capacity. The response of those caring for the infant is usually immediate, which results in a very satisfied baby.

A newborn Christian usually does not know how to study the Word of God or where to find helpful tools to assist in his studying. The hunger for knowledge is there, and the opportunity is often there, but the believer's wisdom for approach to profitable studying has not been developed. One of the most important considerations for the baby believer at this stage is to be involved with a support group of other believers in all growth stages. The purpose of this group is to study the Bible, beginning with the foundational tenets of the faith and progressing to transformation of this foundational truth by the Holy Spirit for the outward growth of each individual believer. A Bible study with an inductive approach, studying verse by verse from general observation to specific interpretation, involving homework and accountability for daily study at a level appropriate for all stages of growth, is definitely warranted for a new believer.

Newborn Babes Need a Mother to Bring Things Close Because They Can't See Too Far
A newborn baby is completely dependent upon its mother to provide everything needed for survival and proper growth in order to progress successfully through the human growth stages. At this stage, everything is cozy and comfortable for the baby as his various needs are met.

At birth, babies can't see as well as older children or adults, and their eyes and visual system aren't yet fully developed. Significant improvement usually occurs during the first few months of life. Up to about three months of age, babies' eyes do not focus on objects more than eight to ten inches from their face or the distance to the parent's face. As the eyes continue to develop during the initial months of life, babies should begin to follow moving objects with their eyes and reach for things at around three months of age.[4]

Babies need someone to bring things close into their ocular range in order to see them clearly. This need is another example of the baby's dependency on another person to assist in its growth and development.

A newborn Christian will benefit from a "spiritual mother" to direct him to useful tools of study, be available to answer questions, and provide suggestions for which Bible study might be appropriate. The individual's inherent characteristics and gifts as ordained by the Lord will determine the pursuit and direction of study. In Ephesians 2:10 we read, "For we are his workmanship, created in Christ Jesus unto good works, which God hath before ordained that we should walk in them." God is faithful to provide discernment to the newborn babe in Christ by the work of the Holy Spirit for the actual beginning of the works He has already planned in that believer's life. Usually, however, God also provides more mature believers to assist the newborn in beholding the spiritual direction through exposure to the Word through study, prayer, and wisdom. As the newborn believer is directed by the Holy Spirit who is teaching that individual through the assistance of mature believers, exposure to the truth of the Word, and circumstances that move the babe through spiritual growth, a response of awe and safety can occur. Examples of the relationship between the newborn believer and God include immediate answers to prayer, an environment of excitement and peace in everyday circumstances, and a sense that God is working everything out satisfactorily in the life of the believer.

In summary, the "newborn babe" is dependent upon his mother and those around him to provide for his basic needs of nourishment, love, and immediate care to grow, because he is unable to feed himself. A new believer needs a "spiritual mother" as directed by the Holy Spirit to assist in the provision of the sincere milk of the Word to grow through the renewal of his mind as he is being transformed into the image of Jesus Christ.

Little Children

Transitioning from newborn babes to little children, we need to look at the supporting Scriptures for this stage of spiritual growth. 1 John 2:1–2, 12 states, "My little children, these things write I unto you, that ye sin not. And if any man sin, we have an advocate with the Father, Jesus Christ, the righteous. And he is the propitiation for our sins: and not for ours only, but also for the sins of the whole world. I write unto you, little children, because your sins are forgiven you for his name's sake."

The spiritual characteristics of this second growth stage are that little children must realize they are forgiven of their sins, they focus on themselves and their surroundings, they have more written to them, they need clear and gentle repetition, they are tossed to and fro by every wind of doctrine, their cozy life has been upset, and they focus on the power of Satan.

Little Children Must Realize They Are Forgiven of Their Sins

Have you ever watched a young child disobey a parental directive by going outside the permitted boundaries? In this particular scenario, one of the house rules is to ask permission prior to leaving the home. Johnny, a six-year-old, active boy, has a friend named Tommy who lives on the next street over. Tommy is often disobedient to his own parents, who have no defined boundaries for behavior, and may be a poor influence on Johnny. The rule for obtaining permission to leave the home is not to be mean or interfere with Johnny's relationship with his friends, but for protection from potential harm existing in the world. If a parent is aware of where and with whom his child is, that enables the child to have a sense of safety by knowing that his parents care. Now Johnny wants to go see Tommy, but his mother is busy vacuuming upstairs. Johnny reasons that he doesn't want to bother his mother and it won't hurt just to go over and see Tommy for a few minutes. Later Johnny returns home to find his mother frantically searching for him. She reminds Johnny that he did not request permission to leave home. He realizes his disobedience and says, "I'm sorry." His mother shows Johnny love without being judgmental, but reminds him that he needs to be disciplined for his disobedience. She tells Johnny that he will not be able to play with Tommy for a week. Over the next few hours, Johnny repeatedly informs his mother how sorry he is, because he doesn't understand that the issue has been dealt with and that his mother does not have any remaining concerns at the moment. Many times, little children will commit the same infractions, repeatedly followed by "I'm sorry," not understanding that they must have a change in the direction of their behavior.

Referring again to 1 John 2:1–2, 12, very young Christians often have a difficult time understanding the forgiveness of their sins through the finished work of the Lord Jesus Christ on the cross. They may often repeat sinful behavior and become convicted by the Holy Spirit to ask forgiveness. This misunderstanding is part of spiritual maturity and will be overcome through the renewing of the mind by the work of the Holy Spirit during progressive sanctification. The importance of being surrounded by more mature believers becomes apparent by assisting the young child to focus upon the truths of God's Word. As a little child walks in the truth beheld at any particular point in time, the fruit of faith becomes more visible, and the influences of the world are discerned more readily. In Romans 10:17 the truth of growing in faith emerges, "So then faith cometh by hearing, and hearing by the word of God."

Little Children Focus on Themselves and Their Surroundings

When you observe young children playing when they don't think anyone is watching, notice how they relate to their proximal environment. Everything is reflected in their perception of how it concerns their own interests. They play with a toy as if no one else is there, or if they interact with another child, the focus is on their interest in the object of play as they seek to control the situation.

We often observe young children who are naturally petulant, noisy, and self-centered. Each person is born with himself in the center of the universe, an impression often reinforced by parents who cater constantly to their young babies. But babies grow into toddlers, and toddlers become children. Sometime during this transition, parents have to use wisdom to teach their children that they are part of a family. For a family to function successfully, there must be clearly defined rules and stated expectations for everyone to follow.[5]

Similarly, young Christians will be intent upon what God will do for them, rather than thinking of serving others. Their focus in church may be on how the sermon will minister to them, what they will get out of it, or what other parishioners will do for them. A little child will be thinking of his own spiritual needs and not even notice what someone else may be enduring. All of this said, this behavior is a normal part of spiritual growth and is in no way indicative of reaping condemnation from other believers. An appropriate Scripture to apply to a little Christian child focusing on themselves is Philippians 2:21, "For all seek their own, not the things which are Jesus Christ's." Conversely at this point in the young believer's walk, a Scripture such as Philippians 2:4, "Look not every man on his own things, but every man also on the things of others," may not resonate, but the seeds of truth will be planted for future watering at a more mature stage of growth.

Little Children Have More Written to Them

When we look at the books written to small children at the library or the bookstore, there are a myriad to choose from. Children are just beginning to read, and a whole new world is opening up to them.

Encyclopaedia Britannica reports that children's literature is "the body of written works and accompanying illustrations produced in order to entertain or instruct young people. This genre encompasses a wide range of works, including acknowledged classics of world literature, picture books and easy-to-read stories written exclusively for children, and fairy tales, lullabies, fables, folk songs, and other primarily orally transmitted materials."[6]

In the book of 1 John, little children have several Scriptures addressed to them regarding biblical truth necessary to behold for growth at this point. In addition to 1 John 2:1–2, 12, there are three additional Scriptures in 1 John written to little children. The first is 2:13c: "I write to you little children because you have known the Father." This Scripture confirms that the little children have been redeemed through forgiveness of sins and have a relationship with God. The second Scripture is 2:18: "Little children, it is the last time: and as ye have heard that antichrist shall come, even now are there many antichrists; whereby we know that it is the last time." The third Scripture is 2:28: "And now, little children, abide in him; that, when he shall appear, we may have confidence, and not be ashamed before him at his coming." This Scripture is advising the little children to focus on the Lord and be ready for His coming, because currently they are focused on looking within themselves.

Little Children Need Clear and Gentle Repetition

Being clear is an essential skill for successful parenting. Children should know exactly what is expected of them. They should know the rules, and they should know what will happen if the rules aren't followed. In a Christian home, they should know that a parent's word is derived from the Word of God. With clarity, your children will learn to listen. In other words, parents should convey what they mean. If you want your child to do something, especially when you are trying to teach better listening skills, you'd better be clear the first time. Not "Why don't you clean your room?" or "How many times do I have to tell you to clean your room?" but a very direct command: "Go clean your room now." That isn't mean. It's clear. Repeating and threatening only dilutes your message and gets your child used to *not* listening to you the first time.[5]

Also, gentleness is paramount for a parent's attitude. With a harsh parental spirit, the child will have a tendency to tune out the parent's words, causing strife and lack of obedience. Looking at the Scriptures Proverbs 15:1, "A soft answer turneth away wrath: but grievous words stir up anger," and Ephesians 6:4, "And, ye fathers, provoke not your children to wrath: but bring them up in the nurture and admonition of the Lord," we see wisdom and guidance from the Word of God.

A spiritual "little child" may have had some exposure to the Scriptures growing up in a Christian home or may have had very little interaction if the home did not honor God. Either way, the new believer must be immersed in the Word of God in order to mature. Each time a truth is studied, whether with a Bible study, through a sermon at church, by individual study, or even conversationally, the young child is hearing the Word of God repeatedly.

This gentle repetition must be clearly and directly taught at the spiritual growth level of the young child. An experienced teacher will be able to discern the receptivity of the young believer and guide this susceptible one slowly in the areas of God's Word as the Lord leads.

Little Children Are Tossed to and fro by Every Wind of Doctrine

When a child goes to school, the influence of a teacher may have a strong effect to alter the course of his life positively or negatively. Usually if the child likes the teacher, he will believe what is taught often without questioning the validity of the content. Conversely, if the child has poor rapport with a teacher, even excellent content may be ignored as being inaccurate or irrelevant.

Positive or negative influences on the students in the classroom were examined in *Healing Classrooms*. Possible interventions were considered related to these positive and negative teacher influences. Five of the examples presented are listed below:

"Possible Interventions on the Part of the Teacher that *Positively* Influence Student Well-Being include:

- *Sense of Belonging*: Educational structure where children and youth feel included
- *Sense of Control*: Opportunities to apply knowledge and skills to real-life situations
- *Feelings of Self-Worth*: Recognize, encourage and praise children and youth

- *Personal Attachments*: Recruit teachers who can form appropriate caring relationships with children and who, as leaders in their communities, support families and others to care for children
- *Intellectual Stimulation*: Enhance child development by providing a variety of educational experiences

Possible Interventions on the Part of the Teacher that *Negatively* Influence Student Well-Being include:

- *Sense of Belonging*: Failure to recognize individual children and youth and to help them feel a part of a "learning community" in the class or school
- *Sense of Control*: Unpredictable and erratic classroom management-with irregular disciplinary methods
- *Feelings of Self-Worth*: Derisive or discriminatory comments to individuals or to groups of children and youth
- *Personal Attachments*: Teachers who are cruel, detached and/or unbothered by the children's overall well-being
- *Intellectual Stimulation*: Repetitive lessons and never-changing teaching style that does not engage the students in active learning" [7]

Therefore, a teacher's influence may be very crucial to the development of a student to avoid confusion and vacillation of character.

Correspondingly, biblical teaching of a Christian in the little children growth stage must be "rightly divided" in a way to present the truth in love, clearly, as the young believer is renewed in his mind. The more someone hears the Scriptures, the deeper they are rooted in the "inner man" for the Holy Spirit to transform the Christian. If the young Christian is exposed to several teachings initially without sufficient guidance and time to assimilate the content, he may continuously change directions in his belief of what the Bible teaches.

The Bible is very clear about the results of young, progressive growth in the doctrines and tenets of the faith. In Ephesians 4:14 we read, "That we henceforth be no more children tossed to and fro, and carried about with every wind of doctrine, by the sleight of men and cunning craftiness, whereby they lie in wait to deceive." This Scripture is the stipulation for evidence of spiritual growth concerning the seven preceding scriptures in Ephesians chapter 4 as related to the gifts available to the Body of Christ and the reason we have them. The contrast presented is to *not* be like a young child tossed to and fro with every wind of doctrine.

The admonition in this particular Scripture in Ephesians 4 is exemplified by a young believer, whom we will call Andy, who listens to a sermon regarding a particular topic in the Word of God. He is excited about the new information and immediately embraces this revelation as truth. The next week Andy hears a podcast on the identical topic but with a totally different and opposing interpretation, and now he is convinced that this explanation is the correct teaching.

For example, in a sermon Andy's pastor explains that each individual decides when the time is right to accept the Lord as Savior. He states that the gospel must be presented, but the individual has a free will to accept or reject the gift of salvation. Our young believer, Andy, sits in the congregation and excitedly accepts this interpretation, because to him it resonates with the experience he recently encountered when the Lord Jesus became his Savior.

The next week, however, Andy listens to a podcast of a well-known pastor who states that God has chosen us in him before the foundation of the world and our salvation is totally orchestrated by a sovereign God as a gift of faith. The individual being dead in their sins has no real choice, but is drawn by the working of the Holy Spirit to accept the Lord Jesus Christ as Savior. Andy thinks, "This famous preacher must know what he is talking about. I think this must be the correct interpretation about conversion."

Paul is actually exhorting the more mature believer *not* to be confused by the different presentations of the Scriptures, "but speaking the truth in love, may grow up into him in all things, which is the head, even Christ." Ephesians 4:15 directs the believer to the Lord Jesus Christ. Andy will grow to this next stage in God's perfect timing for his life.

Little Children Have Their Cozy Life Upset

When a baby comes into the house, everyone's life changes. Now there is a precious little person requiring constant care. Often when the new family goes visiting with their beloved infant, there is no lack of attention, as everyone competes to hold and cuddle the cute little person.

As the child grows up, however, the novelty wears off, and friends and family express their love in other ways. The holding and cuddling changes to talking, playing, and observing the child. Instead of being confined to small areas of a crib, blanket, or proximal environment, the child begins to explore outside or at the playground. The watchful eye of the parent is not as continuous as when the child was a baby. This allows small hurts and altercations with other children to occur as a normal part of interaction.

The secure and cozy life of the baby in which every need and whim was previously attended to now becomes unsettling as the child must adapt to the uncertainties of life. No matter how much a parent is watching a child, there are times when simply looking elsewhere may result in an unfortunate occurrence in the child's life.

In an article written in December 2014 exploring research on injury prevention in children, Morrongiello and McArthur wrote that the relationship between supervision and injury risk "has been hampered by the difficulty of measuring supervision in scientifically rigorous ways." They examined several articles and concluded regarding the available evidence "that mothers and fathers are more similar than different in supervising young children, but that sibling supervision is more lax than parental practices and this contributes to elevated risk for young supervisees when supervised by older siblings." [8]

So, no matter how much or by whom a child is supervised, there is always a potential risk for danger. Since a child can't be placed in a strictly inhibited environment, life's challenges are used to mature the child through all stages of physical growth.

When a person first receives the Lord Jesus Christ as Savior, life can appear to be smooth and comfortable. As the spiritual babe matures, the cozy environment provided by the family of God, immediately answered prayer, and gentle trials quickly changes. The young believer may wonder to where the close relationship with God has departed. Life has now become more difficult in relation to that secure and cozy existence. The question is often, "Where did you go, God?" or "Why do I feel like my prayers are not being answered?" In reality God has gone nowhere but is introducing more difficult trials to continue with a believer's progressive sanctification process of being conformed to the image of Jesus Christ. When more difficult circumstances enter into a believer's life, the course of action will usually drive the individual to delve into the Word of God in order to find the comfort or direction. Hopefully a more mature believer will be sought to guide and counsel the young believer, directing them to study a passage of Scripture that will elicit a response ultimately leading to further study.

Little Children Focus on the Power of Satan

In response to a parent's question regarding dealing with his child's fear of monsters under the bed, Dr. William Sears discussed nighttime fears in this way: "Nighttime can be a scary time for children! Your son is at the age when his vivid imagination is developing, and nightmares can be frequent: Preschoolers often distort reality during sleep and in their dreams. For example, a funny cartoon character your child saw during the day may be morphed into a monster during a dream." [9]

He further recommended that parents should not blame themselves for the child's fear; the bad dreams do not reflect an underlying emotional or psychological problem. Sears suggests a few techniques to deal with the fears:

The first step is to turn the problem into an opportunity for the child to manage the fear and build up the trust between parent and child.

The next strategy is to acknowledge the fear rather than ignoring or devaluing the very real fear with platitudes about acting like a big boy and not a baby. These platitudes will instill in the child that something is wrong with him, and he will not want to confide about other issues. The correct response is to discuss how these fears are a part of growing up and never use the fears in statements concerning discipline, such as "The boogeyman will get you tonight if you scream at Mommy like that."

An additional step is to draw out the child's fears by talking about the imaginary monster and even drawing a picture to demonstrate respect and empathy for the fears.

Also, the parent should track the fear trigger by reducing scary stories or TV that may cause a fearful reaction, including news stories and cartoons if the monster in the drawings resembles a certain character.

Next the parent should not chase the monster away by looking under the bed or in the closet and telling the monster to go away. This may cause distrust due to dishonesty or cause the child to believe that a monster really does exist.

A very important issue is to tell the truth by stipulating that monsters are pretend characters on TV or in storybooks to separate real from imaginary characters.

Finally, a parent should make nighttime a less scary environment, perhaps by suggesting the child need not sleep alone, but maybe in a "special place" at the foot of the parents' bed for a week, and not waking up Mommy and Daddy, because they need sleep too.

Just as a human child may be growing through a "monster stage," a young Christian child is growing through increasingly more difficult trials that often evoke fear and isolation, that may be quite different from a feeling of comfort experienced during the "newborn babe" stage. The amount of exposure to the Word of God and time spent in prayer to burgeon a developing relationship with the Lord will cause the believer to focus more on spiritual truths. This relationship helps to create an opportunity for the young Christian to be transformed from his fear and build up the trust between him and his Savior. At this juncture of the Christian's walk, the focus may be on the "prince of the power of the air" as the cause of everything. This is tantamount to looking behind every bush for Satan to jump out and attack. Unlike the monsters under the bed that need to be dispelled, Satan is very real. 1 Peter 5:8: "Be sober, be vigilant, because your adversary the devil, as a roaring lion, walketh about, seeking whom he may devour." A believer definitely needs to be aware of the enemy, but vigilance is keeping a careful watch for possible danger or difficulties, not being paranoid and totally focused on Satan. The apostle John addresses the young child regarding the reality of the evil one in the world in 1 John 2:18: "Little children, it is the last time: and as ye have heard that antichrist shall come, even now are there many antichrists; whereby we know that it is the last time."

The little Christian child may assign more power to Satan than he actually has. Satan was a created being and is under God's sovereign power. Isaiah 14:12 refers to Satan as "Lucifer, son of the morning and fallen from heaven" due to a proud heart, making statements in verses 13 and 14 such as "I will ascend into heaven. I will exalt my throne above the stars of God. I will sit also upon the mount of the congregation, in the sides of the north. I will ascend above the heights of the clouds. I will be like the most High." We see in Job 1:12 that Satan must seek permission from God for the extent of torment he may exert: "And the Lord said unto Satan, behold all that he hath is in thy power; only upon himself put not forth thine hand."

As the Christian in the "young child" stage is being tossed to and fro by every wind of doctrine, it's understandable why he might focus on Satan intensely. In the Scriptures, we read in 2 Corinthians 11:13–14, "For such are false apostles, deceitful workers, transforming themselves into the apostles of Christ. And no marvel; for Satan himself is transformed into an angel of light." He is constantly learning through sermons, Bible studies, and prayer that the possibility of deceit always exists to draw him away from the truth into a false doctrine.

In summary, we may see many "little children" in our churches. These are the believers who constantly question that their sins are forgiven, are very self-focused on their own walk with the Lord, and have more exhortations and doctrinal truths written to them; they need to be sitting under the "rightly divided" truth and hearing it multiple times and in various ways. They are susceptible to being influenced by different doctrines, their stable life of comfort is changed as they begin the walk through more difficult trials, and their focus may be on the fearful and evil reality of Satan, not on the God of the universe.

Romans 8:1 tells us that "there is therefore now no condemnation to them which are in Christ Jesus, who walk not after the flesh, but after the Spirit." Those in Christ have been redeemed by the death of Jesus Christ on the cross. We will examine the depth of being "in Christ" in chapter 6. For now, we accept where the little children are in their spiritual walk as being exactly where the sovereign Lord has them. As the "little child" beholds that his sins are truly forgiven, he transitions into the next growth stage.

Young Men

The "little child" has been growing through many trials, falling down and getting back up as he is learning to walk in the truth being studied. Now we need to proceed to the next stage of growth that occurs as we continue to mature in our walk with the Lord.

Let's look carefully at how this tree in the illustration exemplifies the root/ fruit principle. The apostle Paul used this principle in his epistles to present the doctrine or root in the earlier chapters and demonstrate the growth or fruit manifested in the life of a believer in the later chapters.

Refer to chart 5 in the appendix: "Union with Christ as a Small Seed." Beginning with our union with Jesus Christ at salvation, or justifying sanctification, we look at the roots of the tree as depicted in the illustration with the outline of the Bible. The small seed from which the tree has grown represents our new life with Jesus Christ as Savior. Our growth, which commenced at salvation, continues with studying the Word of God, which renews our mind in truth. The result of this renewal of the mind is our progressive sanctification, which involves constantly setting down "spiritual roots" to anchor us in our faith and help us in our moment-by-moment walk with the Lord Jesus Christ. Contained in the roots of the tree, the book of Romans is used to exemplify the doctrines of our faith as the apostle Paul develops them in chapters 1–11. Specifically represented in this example are salvation, justification, redemption, sanctification, and the attributes of God. We refer to these first eleven chapters of Romans as the root, or inward renewal of the believer from the truth in God's Word. Romans chapters 12–16 expound upon the fruit, or outward manifestation of the renewed "inner man" of the Christian. Also, other Scriptures are listed under "growth" that help the reader to understand the fruit principle.

Notice the difference in the size of the fruit on the tree. This corresponds to the different levels of growth in the Christian's fruit bearing. For instance, the believer may manifest obedience more consistently than self-control. We will see more mature fruit in the young man than we saw in the little child or the newborn babe. This is not because the young man tries harder or works at it more, but because the young man has grown to the stage where he is now beholding the sovereignty of God in his life and focusing more on the ministering to the saints rather than what God is doing for him personally.

Young Men Have Overcome the Wicked One

Ideally, as a young human man matures, he is leaving behind the careless, self-centered life and is focusing more on the needs of others as he contemplates his future related to employment, stability, and settling down with a wife and children. Gone are the impulsive antics that define boyhood and self-indulgence. Now, the reality of sustaining a productive life becomes very important.

In the developing human brain, areas that specialize in language grow rapidly until about age thirteen and then cease to grow. The frontal lobes of the brain are responsible for high-level reasoning and decision making; these areas aren't fully mature until the early twenties, Deborah Yurgelun-Todd, a neuroscientist at Harvard's Brain Imaging Center, says. As the immature part of the child's brain is being assimilated and the more developed adult brain is not yet completed, there is an "in-between" time. The young men at this time may be informed, but they are not yet prepared.[10]

Tim Elmore, founder and president of Growing Leaders (GrowingLeaders. com), an international nonprofit organization created to develop emerging leaders, defines the seven marks of maturity:

1. A mature person is able to keep long-term commitments; delayed gratification is operative to continue to do the right thing even when the person doesn't necessarily desire to at the moment.
2. A mature person is unshaken by flattery or criticism; compliments or criticism don't affect the security of their identity.
3. A mature person possesses a spirit of humility; thinking of yourself less and others more by not drawing attention to yourself and giving honor to the Creator who has bestowed the talent. This attitude is the antithesis of arrogance.
4. A mature person's decisions are based on character, not feelings; values and principles guide their decisions rather than reacting to life's options and being proactive with a strong character.
5. A mature person expresses gratitude consistently; immature children assume they deserve whatever good happens to them, while mature people appreciate what they have compared to others.
6. A mature person knows how to prioritize others before themselves; the route from childhood to maturity is to forgo your own desires and seek to meet the needs of less fortunate people.
7. A mature person seeks wisdom before acting; rather than believing they have all the answers, they accept counsel and learn from others such as teachers, parents, and coaches.[10]

In 1 John 2:13, the young man is addressed in this way: "I write unto you, young men, because ye have overcome the wicked one." Growing from not realizing the forgiveness of God in the "little children" stage and focusing on the power of Satan to beholding the sovereignty of God over the power of Satan, the young man is maturing in the truth of the Word of God. This transitional growth is depicted in Psalm 1:3: "like a tree planted by the rivers of water, that bringeth forth his fruit in his season; his leaf also shall not wither; and whatsoever he doeth shall prosper."

Young Men Are Strong, and the Word of God Abides in Them

As the young man grows in grace and knowledge of the Lord Jesus Christ, trials are experienced at a more difficult level of persecution. A believer's level of maturity is nourished by his relationship with the Lord, which has come from studying God's Word, prayer, and the transformation by the Holy Spirit. The Scriptures Colossians 3:16-6–17, "Let the word of Christ dwell in you richly in all wisdom; teaching and admonishing one another in psalms and hymns and spiritual songs, singing with grace in your hearts to the Lord. And whatsoever ye do in word or deed, do all in the name of the lord Jesus, giving thanks to God and the Father by him," refers to a mature believer who has walked with the Lord in a close relationship. In order for the word of Christ to dwell richly in a believer, he must spend time studying the Bible with an open heart and mind, "rightly dividing" the Scriptures. The Greek word for "dwell" is *eniokeo*, which means "to inhabit," and the verb tense is present imperative active, which is a command for continuous or repeated action. The sense of Paul's exhortation is to continue to study as you already are doing. We need to encourage each other in the Body of Christ to continue on with the often difficult but very rewarding and joyous life in Christ.

At this point in the maturation process, the believer is more interested in serving others with the emerging gifts "differing according to the grace that is given to us" (Rom. 12:6), rather than being concerned with "what is God doing in my life." I believe this mature spiritual attitude is related to the renewed mind in the sovereignty of God in most every aspect of life. Romans 12:1–2 exemplifies this truth: "I beseech you therefore, brethren, by the mercies of God, that ye present your bodies a living sacrifice, holy, acceptable unto God, which is your reasonable service. And be not conformed to this world: but be ye transformed by the renewing of your mind, that ye may prove what is that good, and acceptable, and perfect will of God."

The offering of the body as a living sacrifice comes as a maturing fruit at a point where you see the hand of God in control of every circumstance, trial, and relationship; the reasonable service is growing forward as the walk of the believer is centered on the Lord Jesus Christ more than on self. All of this is a result of the renewed mind through the transformation of the Holy Spirit for the glory of God.

In summary, young men have beheld the sovereignty of God in life's circumstances and trials by realizing that Satan does not hold the power over them or God. They also are able to withstand spiritual warfare due to strength and power obtained from the Lord as they are renewed in truth and the Word of God abides in them richly. At this stage, we see a strength that holds fast, but there is more growth coming to reach a level of maturity that is rich in the fruit of the Spirit with a relationship to God that is steadfast and time honored.

Fathers

This last growth stage is achieved by the believers who have grown to the highest level of maturity. They are not praised because of their greatness, but are more revered due to their humility and solid, moment-by-moment walk in the grace and sovereignty of the Lord Jesus Christ.

Fathers Have Known God from the Beginning

In an article regarding essential fathering skills, Keith Zafren wrote that it's important for moms and dads to know the essential skills a father can master to do the following:

1. enhance relationships with their children (It's never too late to bring about better communication and more compassion between father and child.)
2. teach and mentor the next generation
3. be a good fathering role model and help prepare children for their own adult lives and parenting [11]

Parents often make mistakes, but their desire should be to raise their children to be ready to take the baton and succeed in the next generation. Teaching takes wisdom, experience, and proximity to the child the parent is trying to nurture.

A father in the faith is described this way in 1 John 2:13–14: "I have written unto you, fathers, because ye have known him that is from the beginning." We know that "him" in this verse is referring to God, the only one who existed before time. "In the beginning God created the heaven and the earth" (Gen. 1:1). We see God from the beginning also in John 1:1: "In the beginning was the Word, and the Word was with God, and the Word was God." This verse is also referring to God the Son, the Lord Jesus Christ who is God.

Fathers Behold God's Sovereignty and Walk in That Truth

The myriad of challenges that experienced fathers report to be the most important and examples of their best advice are as follows:

1. Fatherhood is about growing up and accepting responsibility, which requires devotion of time to the children rather than always pursuing self-centered goals.
2. The rewards for investment into fatherhood exceed the sacrifices as each parent finds his or her unique way to relate to the issues concerning the children.
3. Choices that are made, while developing trust for instincts in parenting skills, will reflect the uniqueness of strengths and competencies in the parents learning to care for babies.
4. Talking to other parents who have experience may facilitate the creativity and stamina that men and women bring to parenting. Sharing experiences will often assist in gaining a new perspective and different ways of assisting in taking care of the family.
5. Maintaining good health and mental well-being and an attitude of taking each day as it comes, rather than being overwhelmed by the responsibility of fatherhood, will be helpful when the mistakes occur.[12]

As a mature father in the faith relates to younger believers, we observe his devotion to the Lord Jesus Christ and the fruit bearing in his daily walk. In Colossians 2:6–7 we read, "As ye have therefore received Christ Jesus the Lord, so walk ye in him. Rooted and built up in him, and stablished in the faith, as ye have been taught, abounding therein with thanksgiving." These Scriptures relate to the walk of the believer by faith. We received Jesus Christ as Lord by faith as we see in Ephesians 2:8–9: "For by grace are ye saved through faith: and that not of yourselves: it is the gift of God. Not of works, lest any many should boast."

We walk the same way by faith. God has given us the faith to believe, and He will give us the faith to serve Him as "his workmanship created in Christ Jesus unto good works, which God hath before ordained that we should walk in them" (Eph. 2:10). What a comfort to know that God has ordered our steps before the world began and that He will give us discernment as to the direction they take.

The most mature church recorded in the New Testament is found in the book of Philippians, as penned by the apostle Paul under the inspiration of the Holy Spirit. If we desire to glean the essence of a mature father, a careful scrutiny of Philippians will reveal God's truth regarding maturity to the dedicated student of the Word. Let's examine a few of these Scriptures beginning with Philippians 1:9–11: "And I pray that your love may abound yet more and more in knowledge and in all judgment; That ye may approve things that are excellent; that ye may be sincere and without offense till the day of Christ; Being filled with the fruits of righteousness, which are by Jesus Christ, unto the glory and praise of God."

Unpacking these verses, we see that Paul's desire as a father of the faith is that the fruit of love may be very abundant in the lives of the believers in the Philippian church. Not just for gaining more knowledge, but to attain the ability to discern truth and knowledge through the agape love of God shed abroad in our hearts by the Holy Spirit. When we are approving things that are excellent, this does not mean good versus evil, but examining two very godly elements and discerning the direction in which God is leading. By looking to the more excellent way, we are maturing and keeping our focus upon the Lord Jesus Christ and walking in the truth we know to serve and glorify God. The "fruits of righteousness" refer to the outward manifestation of believers' behavior as we are transformed by the renewing of our mind as reflected by "Christ in us the hope of glory" found in Colossians 1:27.

The book of 2 Timothy is essential for understanding the relationship of a mature father to a young son in the faith. The apostle Paul is very close to death and has a desire to pass the major tenets of the faith to exhort Timothy. (Please refer to chapter 1 for more detail regarding the six components of exhortation related to a follower of the Lord Jesus Christ.) Paul's exhortation to Timothy as a maturing pastor in 2 Timothy 4: 1–4 is "I charge thee therefore before God, and the Lord Jesus Christ, who shall judge the quick and the dead at his appearing and his kingdom; Preach the word; be instant in season, out of season; reprove, rebuke, exhort with all longsuffering and doctrine. For the time will come when they will not endure sound doctrine; but after their own lusts shall they heap to themselves teachers having itching ears; And they shall turn away their ears from the truth, and shall be turned unto fables."

You are encouraged to study extensively the book of 2 Timothy to have a mature perspective of the relationship of a father in the faith mentoring a son in the faith gifted by God in the same manner. In this particular case, the gift is one of a pastor. Everyone in the Body of Christ needs someone both older and younger to counsel, exhort, and come alongside in times of need.

In summary, the Christian growth stage of father is the most mature of the believers found in the Body of Christ. They remain strong in their Christian walk by transformation of the Word of God, behold the sovereignty of God to the extent of standing firm in adversity, think more highly of others related to a ministry perspective, and are able to mentor younger believers with discernment, wisdom, and experience. We need to remember, however, that these fathers are not perfect, as only our Lord Jesus Christ walked this earth without sin; 2 Corinthians 5:21: "For he hath made him to be sin for us, who knew no sin; that we might be made the righteousness of God in him." Unfortunately, we do not see many fathers in the Body of Christ today, which may be due to the lack of "rightly dividing" the word in many of our churches.

Summarizing chapter 5, there are four stages a Christian will grow through in his walk with the Lord. Each believer passes through these stages at a rate determined by God's sovereign plan and for His glory. The way a Christian grows is not in his own effort, but by the transformation of his inner man by the work of the Holy Spirit. As Paul admonished Timothy to "study to show thyself approved unto God, a workman that needeth not to be ashamed, rightly dividing the word of truth" in 2 Timothy 2:15, we all need to be in the Word to learn about the God we serve.

Alice Buffington and Heather Cook

We met Alice and Heather in chapter 2. At this point in the book, you should read the chapter again to refresh your understanding of the characteristics and spiritual walk of each of these women.

Next, you want to compare their lives to the four growth stages as delineated in this chapter. An important caveat to remember is that, while believers will progress through these growth stages, there may occur an overlapping from one stage to another, as the believer exhibits characteristics from both stages. For instance, a believer who desires the sincere milk of the Word, wants to study the Word, is growing rapidly, and is beginning to experience trials that are becoming more difficult and upsetting their cozy life is transitioning between the newborn babe and little children stages.

Think about what you have discerned in this chapter, and assign Alice and Heather to the appropriate growth stages based upon your perception of where they are in their spiritual walks with the Lord Jesus Christ.

Questions for Group Discussion or Individual Study

1. Using chart 4 and the explanations of each growth stage, explain in your own words the characteristics of each stage. In which stage do you see yourself? Your family members? Your friends?

2. After you have decided which stage best describes your walk with the Lord, ask someone who knows you well if they agree with your answer. Discuss any differences.

3. Think about individuals in the Bible and how they are portrayed. What stage of growth would you assign to Peter, Paul, Timothy?

4. Explain why a spiritual newborn babe can't feed himself.

5. Explain why a spiritual newborn babe needs a mother to bring things in close.

6. Explain why a spiritual little child focuses on the power of Satan.

7. Explain why a spiritual young man is strong and abiding in the Word of God.

8. Have you ever heard anyone teach about these growth stages of a Christian before? What were the similarities? What were the differences?

9. Do you know anyone personally who would be considered a father of the faith? Why? If not, are there any other Christians you could use as examples from biographies you have read? Or any current biblical leaders?

10. What have you learned about examining Christian growth from the perspective of progressive sanctification? How will that affect your study of God's Word?

6

Where Do We Go from Here with Our Christian Growth?

For in him dwelleth all the fullness of the Godhead bodily.

—Colossians 2:9

And ye are complete in him, which is the head of all principality and power.

—Colossians 2:10

A common statement from the pulpit sometimes heard during a sermon or at the end of a prayer is "Lord, I am just a sinner saved by grace." This phrase seems to be innocuous enough, but part of the purpose of this chapter is to change the perspective of that phrase by careful scrutiny of what the depth of our relationship with the Lord Jesus Christ actually encompasses. By the end of this chapter, my prayer is for you to behold the perspective that we are saints saved by grace who are still capable of sinning.

Before we examine who we are *in Christ*, we need to review how we arrive at this point. We won't exhaust the doctrines of salvation, justification, sanctification, and glorification, but just focus on the finished work of Jesus Christ in our lives.

In order to be directed to an understanding of what the Lord Jesus Christ has accomplished, the first step is to examine the Scriptures. God has provided for us in His Word the answer to any questions we may have, with the caveat as explored in chapter 1 from 2 Timothy 2:15 to "rightly divide the word of truth."

The Gospel

The Greek word for "gospel" used in the New Testament is *euggelion*, which means "a good message." The gospel is defined in 1 Corinthians 15: 3–4 (italics) with a preface in verses 1–2 and the beginning of verse 3: "Moreover, brethren, I declare unto you *the gospel* which I preached unto you, which also ye have received, and wherein ye stand; By which also ye are saved, if ye keep in memory what I preached unto you, unless ye have believed in vain. For I delivered unto you first of all that which I also received, how that *Christ died for our sins according to the scriptures; And that he was buried, and that he rose again the third day according to the scriptures.*"

Validation for any occurrence requires witnesses. The apostle Paul penned the subsequent verses 5–8 to specify how many people saw the risen Lord: "And that he was seen of Cephas, then of the twelve: After that he was seen of above five hundred brethren at once; of whom the greater part remain unto this present, but some are fallen asleep. After that, he was seen of James; then of all the apostles. And last of all he was seen of me also, as one born out of due time." With an account of so many witnesses, there can be no doubt to anyone seeking the truth that the Lord Jesus was seen after His resurrection. Many alternate explanations have been given to deny the bodily resurrection of the Lord Jesus Christ. The first account we have of deceptive reporting following the resurrection is in the book of Matthew 28:11–15:

Now when they were going, behold, some of the watch came into the city, and showed unto the chief priests all the things that were done. And when they were assembled with the elders, and had taken counsel, they gave large money unto the soldiers, Saying, Say ye, His disciples came by night, and stole him away while we slept. And if this come to the governor's ears, we will persuade him, and secure you. So they took the money, and did as they were taught: and this saying is commonly reported among the Jews until this day.

These lies perpetuated in AD 33 are still being propagated today when individuals declare that Jesus Christ was simply a good teacher, a prophet, or a carpenter. By virtue of denying that Jesus Christ rose from the dead, an individual may ignore the truth about his own sin and subsequent separation from God.

Paul made many references to the gospel in his writing, but in two books he refers to "my gospel." In Romans 2:16, he writes, "In the day when God shall judge the secrets of men by Jesus Christ according to *my gospel*," and in Romans

16:25 as a conclusion to this great doctrinal epistle, Paul writes "Now to him that is of power to stablish you according to *my gospel*, and the preaching of Jesus Christ, according to the revelation of the mystery, which was kept secret since the world began." The Greek word used here for "my" is *mou*, which translates to "my or mine own" and makes this gospel preached by Paul very personal.

Other references to the gospel by the apostle Paul include Romans 1:1, "Paul, a servant of Jesus Christ, called to be an apostle, separated unto the gospel of God"; Romans 1:9, "For God is my witness, whom I serve with my spirit in the gospel of His Son that without ceasing I make mention of you always in my prayers"; Romans 1:16, "For I am not ashamed of the gospel of Christ: for it is the power of God unto salvation to every one that believeth; to the Jew first, and also to the Greek"; Ephesians 1:13, "In whom ye also trusted after that ye heard the word of truth, the gospel of your salvation, ye were sealed with that holy Spirit of promise"; and Ephesians 3:6, "That the Gentiles should be fellow heirs, and of the same body, and partakers of his promise in Christ by the gospel." These Scriptures are in no way exhaustive concerning the gospel of Jesus Christ. I encourage you to study each of these scriptures further for context and depth of meaning.

Salvation and the Body of Christ

On the day of Pentecost detailed in Acts chapter 2, the apostle Peter was addressing the nation of Israel regarding the original prophecy of Joel, which was being fulfilled by the outpouring of the Holy Spirit:

> But this is that which was spoken by the prophet Joel, "AND IT SHALL COME TO PASS IN THE LAST DAYS, SAITH GOD, I WILL POUR OUT OF MY SPIRIT UPON ALL FLESH: AND YOUR SONS AND YOUR DAUGHTERS SHALL PROPHESY, AND YOUR YOUNG MEN SHALL SEE VISIONS, AND YOUR OLD MEN SHALL DREAM DREAMS: AND ON MY SERVANTS AND ON MY HANDMAIDENS I WILL POUR OUT IN THOSE DAYS OF MY SPIRIT, AND THEY SHALL PROPHESY." (Acts 2:16–18)

Peter continued talking to the house of Israel about Jesus of Nazareth, his miracles and signs, the One whom the Jews had crucified and slain, and David's prophecies concerning Jesus. Peter finishes his oracle with these scriptures in Acts 2:36–38:

> Therefore let all the house of Israel know assuredly, that God hath made that same Jesus whom ye have crucified, both Lord and Christ. Now when they heard this, they were pricked in their heart, and said unto Peter and to the rest of the apostles, Men and brethren, what shall we do? Then Peter said unto them, Repent, *and* be baptized every one of you in the name of Jesus Christ for the remission of sins, *and* ye shall receive the gift of the Holy Spirit.

Peter was clearly addressing the nation of Israel in these verses. They were convicted in their hearts and cried out to Peter and the other apostles what was to be done. Peter answered them very clearly with a three-step response:

- repent
- be baptized in the name of Jesus Christ for the remission of sins
- then receive the gift of the Holy Spirit

The italicized word "and" in Acts 2:38 referenced above is a conjunction that connects words together. The Greek word for "and" used here is *kai* as a "cumulative force denoting degree by successive addition of words in a progressive format." These three steps, therefore, determine the order of salvation at that point in time. One important aspect of interpretation in the Word is to be aware of what is known by the individuals living during the specific time depicted and how God was dealing specifically with His people.

Fast-forward to Acts 16, in which Paul and Silas had watched a young woman who was possessed with a spirit of divination and who earned her masters much wealth by soothsaying. Paul became grieved by her behavior and commanded the spirit to come out of her. Her masters, becoming angry due to their sudden loss of income, took Paul and Silas before the magistrates, charging them with teaching unlawful customs. Paul and Silas were beaten and cast into prison with instructions given to the jailor to secure them in the stocks. Paul and Silas were praying and singing praises to God while the prisoners were listening intently to them. At midnight, a strong earthquake suddenly rocked the foundations of the prison, and all the doors opened. The jailor woke up and saw that the prison doors were open, and he was about to kill himself, because the penalty for a jailor losing prisoners was to forfeit his own life. Paul cried out that they were all still there, and the jailor was extremely overcome and knelt before Paul and Silas, asking in Acts 16:30, "Sirs, what must I do to be saved?" The answer in verse 31 is "Believe on the Lord Jesus Christ, and thou shalt be saved, and thy house." There is no mention of repentance or baptism in this answer. Paul and Silas spoke the word of the Lord to the household of the jailor, who cleaned up their beaten backs, and then he and his household were baptized with water.

In the book of Ephesians 2:8–9, the scriptures seem to tell a different story. They simply state, "For by grace are ye saved through faith; and that not of yourselves: it is the gift of God. Not of works, lest any man should boast." Salvation comes by faith alone in the finished work of Jesus Christ and not by any human merit or through water baptism.

Let's repeat the three verses together. Acts 2:38: "Repent, and be baptized every one of you in the name of Jesus Christ for the remission of sins, and ye shall receive the gift of the Holy Spirit." Acts 16:31: "Believe on the Lord Jesus Christ, and thou shalt be saved, and thy house." And Ephesians 2:8–9: "For by grace are ye saved through faith; and that not of yourselves: it is the gift of God. Not of works, lest any man should boast." If you study these verses closely, you will notice they are very different scenarios concerning salvation, almost in a progressive way. First repentance and subsequent water baptism in the name of the Lord Jesus Christ, and then the receiving of the Holy Spirit. Next, you just believe on the Lord Jesus Christ for salvation. Finally, you are saved by grace that is a gift from God, and there are no works exercised by the individual because God gets all the glory.

Why is examining these scriptures so important? Are there three different ways to be saved? Is there a contradiction in God's Word? Why do these scriptures, examined together, seem so confusing? The answer is found as the apostle Paul is speaking in Galatians 2:7: "But contrawise, when they saw that the gospel of the uncircumcision was committed unto me as the gospel of the circumcision was unto Peter." The apostle Paul was speaking here not about a different gospel, but about how the gospel was disseminated to two different groups of people. We see that Peter is the apostle to the nation of Israel and Paul is the apostle to the Body of Christ. When studying the books of the Bible written by Paul, we see there is a progression of revelation when they are viewed chronologically.

Refer to chart 6 in the appendix: "Chronological Order of New Testament Books." The accounts of the Lord Jesus, often referred to as the four Gospels, were written from AD 50 to AD 95 but actually occurred during the years AD 30–33. The apostle Paul was saved around AD 35, and the chronological order of the New Testament books, including all of Paul's epistles, are portrayed in the chart. There is a definite comparison between the growth stages of a Christian toward maturity and the content of the early epistles written prior to the section titled "Mystery Revealed." A transitional book between the early writings of Paul and the prison epistles of Ephesians, Philippians, and Colossians when the mystery was totally revealed, is the book of Romans, which contains an elaboration of the essential doctrines of the Christian faith. When the books written after the period of the four Gospels are placed within the book of Acts chronologically, the apparent progressive revelation to Paul is very clear. An adequately detailed study of the entire New Testament is beyond the scope for presentation of spiritual growth as considered in this book, but would be very revealing to anyone who would perform a thorough inductive investigation. As this chapter is developed, however, the crucial topics connecting the spiritual growth of a believer to beholding of the progressive revelation given to the apostle Paul will be unpacked to support our spiritual relationship in the Lord Jesus Christ.

Since the mystery is alluded to by the apostle Paul briefly in the book of Romans and expounded in great detail within the prison epistles, examination of the relationship of this mystery to the Body of Christ is necessary to understand our position as believers in Jesus Christ in this current era of God's plan from eternity past to eternity future.

Looking first at Romans 16:25, we see a reference to the mystery in a benediction to the believers at Rome: "Now to him that is of power to stablish you according to my gospel, and the preaching of Jesus Christ, according to the revelation of the mystery, which was kept secret since the world began." The takeaway from this verse regarding the mystery is that Paul is citing his gospel, declaring that his preaching of this gospel concerning the Lord Jesus Christ is according to the mystery that was revealed to him, and that the mystery has never been revealed from the beginning of time as recorded in the Old Testament until this point in time recorded in the New Testament. This truth clearly supports the progressive revelation given to the apostle Paul.

Looking next in the book of Colossians, we find that the apostle Paul gives an overview of the mystery and its purpose for the Body of Christ. Colossians 1:25–27 states, "Whereof I am made a minister, according to the dispensation of God which is given to me for you, to fulfill the Word of God; Even the mystery which hath been hid from ages and from generations, but now is made manifest to his saints: To whom God would make known what is the riches of the glory of this mystery among the Gentiles; which is Christ in you, the hope of glory."

Examining several words contained in these verses in the original Greek language is imperative for "rightly dividing" the Word of truth. The word "minister" is the Greek word *diakonos*, which means "to run on errands, an attendant, minister, to hasten." We derive the word "deacon" as an office in today's churches from this Greek word. The origin of this relationship is found in Acts 6:1–4 describing Stephen and Philip. They were initially chosen as distributors of alms and became helpers to the apostles, and then evangelists. The care of the churches become dependent upon the deacons who helped the elders. Paul's capacity was to be a minister, not of himself, but according to the dispensation of God, as the next section of the verse stipulates. The Greek for the word "dispensation" is *oikonomia*, "the administration of divine grace which was given to the apostle Paul to fulfill the Word of God." The

Greek word "fulfill" is *pleroo*, meaning "to preach or explain fully." Putting the meanings together to interpret this Scripture we see that the apostle Paul was selected by God to explain the Word of God, and specifically to the Gentiles as we have seen in Galatians 2:7.

In Colossians 1:26 the exact focus of this fulfillment or explanation of the Word of God concerns the mystery which has been hid from ages and generations. The Greek word for "mystery" is *musterion* and refers to "a secret or mystery through the idea of silence imposed by initiation into religious rites" and "a locking up or that which serves for locking up." Other meanings include "in general something hidden or not fully manifest" and "some sacred thing hidden or secret which is naturally unknown to human reason and is only known by the revelation of God." In the writings of Paul, the word *musterion* is sometimes applied in a peculiar sense to the calling of the Gentiles. Paul refers to this mystery that has been hidden with the expectation of being revealed at a particular time. Continuing on in verse 26, the particular time is indicated as *now* being made manifest to God's saints. The simple conjunction "but" is the Greek word *de*, which means "continuative" or "now" and is often unexpressed in the English language. The word "now" is the Greek word *nuni*, which is an adverb indicating time, place, or manner in which its action is accomplished. In this verse, the word "now" means "just now or at this specific time."

Next, we examine "made manifest," which is the Greek word *phaneroo* in the aorist indicative passive tense, expressing action that is not continuous with the subject receiving the action of the verb. This verb tense is extremely important to demonstrate that the revelation of the mystery is one point in time and it is occurring for the first time.

The object of the revelation of the mystery is very important here. Because Paul is an apostle to the Gentiles, we can determine that the saints addressed here are members of the Body of Christ, not the nation of Israel. The word "saints" is *hagios* in the Greek and means "sacred, consecrated to God, sharing in God's purity and abstaining from earth's defilement." God ordained the apostle Paul to reveal this mystery that had been hidden during the time of the Old Testament, during the ministry of the Lord Jesus Christ, and during the early time period in the book of Acts. The people to whom the mystery applied are indicated as the saints in the Body of Christ.

Our next consideration should be the content of the mystery. Verse 27 gives the outpouring of the mystery: "For God to make known the riches of the glory of this mystery among the Gentiles: which is Christ in you, the hope of glory." The word "riches" in the Greek is *ploutos*, meaning "wealth as fullness, possessions, abundant, richness." These riches are to be "made known," or *gnorizo* in the Greek, meaning "to make known, to know, to certify, declare, give to understand." The verb tense used here is aorist infinitive active, which refers to punctiliar action and does not signify the time of action that is accomplished by the subject. The sense of the action is at one point in time. God, defined by the Greek word *theos*, meaning "the supreme deity," is the originator of certification and declaration of the mystery to the saints. The word "would" used before "make known" is important to convey the depth of God's intentions. In the Greek "would" is *thelo*, which indicates "willing something and pressing on to action and denotes elective inclination and love." The verb tense is aorist indicative active, which expresses action that is not continuous and does not specify the relative time of the action to the time of speaking accomplished by the subject. God, of course, is the subject, and He is actually willing actively by His love to impart how wonderful and abundant the riches and glory of the mystery are as directed specifically to the Gentiles.

Next, the actual essence of the mystery needs to be examined. "Glory," or *doxa* in the Greek, is defined as "glory, honour, praise, worship, brightness." Here the splendor and brightness of this mystery imparted only to the Gentiles is declared as "Christ in you the hope of glory." "Gentile," or *ethnos* in the Greek, is defined as "a race, a tribe, a nation." Paul uses this word to distinguish this group of people from the Jews who are called "Laos," the people of God or the Israel of God. "Hope," or *elpis* in the Greek, is defined as "to anticipate, usually with pleasure." Another definition is "the desire of some good with expectation of obtaining it." Also, we see hope as the object of the thing hoped for. This "hope of glory" is for all who believe in the Lord Jesus Christ and enter into the Body of Christ.

As was earlier stated, these verses in Colossians 1:25–27 are an overview of the purpose of the mystery as related to the Body of Christ. To develop the depth of the mystery, we must turn to the book of Ephesians chapter 3.

The specific verses that describe the details of the mystery as revealed by the apostle Paul in his epistles are contained in Ephesians 3:1–11:

1. For this cause I Paul, the prisoner of Jesus Christ for you Gentiles, 2. If ye have heard of the dispensation of the grace of God which is given me to you-ward: 3. How that by revelation he made known unto me the mystery; (as I wrote afore in few words, 4. Whereby, when ye read, ye may understand my knowledge in the mystery of Christ) 5. Which in other ages was not made known unto the sons of men, as it is now revealed unto his holy apostles and prophets by the Spirit; 6. That the Gentiles should be fellow heirs, and of the same body, and partakers of his promise in Christ by the gospel: 7. Whereof I was made a minister, according to the gift of the grace of God given unto me by the effectual working of his power. 8. Unto me, who am less than the least of all saints, is this grace given, that I should preach among the Gentiles the unsearchable riches of Christ; 9. And to make all men see what is the fellowship of the mystery, which from the beginning of the world hath been hid in God who created all things by Jesus Christ: 10. To the intent that now unto the principalities and powers in heavenly places might be known by the church the manifold wisdom of God, 11. According to the eternal purpose which he purposed in Christ Jesus our Lord.

Rather than observe and interpret each verse word by word, the passage in Ephesians 3 will be paraphrased, with specific words defined as necessary for clarification. The reader is encouraged to study these verses in detail as God has directed us through the apostle Paul in 2 Timothy 2:15: "Study to show thyself approved unto God, a workman that needeth not to be ashamed, rightly dividing the word of truth." And as always, the emphasis of study in this verse is to "rightly divide" God's Word.

Referring back to chart 6 in the appendix, "Chronological Order of New Testament Books," you will notice that Ephesians, Philippians, and Colossians were all postulated to be written in AD 63. Ephesians is listed first in the chart because the explanation of the mystery is very detailed in this epistle written by the apostle Paul. In the other two epistles, the mystery is referred to as if the reader already has had a thorough elucidation of its revelation to the Gentiles.

Beginning in Ephesians 3:1, the apostle Paul refers to himself as a prisoner of Jesus Christ for the Gentiles. He is stating the exclusivity of his message to the Gentiles as we have already seen in Galatians 2:7, the writing of which preceded Ephesians by nine years. The church at Ephesus would have been very aware of this truth of his apostleship to the Gentiles.

Next, Paul explains the administration of divine grace, which was given to him for the Gentiles. God actually revealed the mystery to Paul, which he proclaimed as being manifested at this particular point in time and was not known before. The mystery has three components, which are listed by Paul in Ephesians 3:6. The *first component of the mystery* states that the Gentiles should be fellow heirs. Prior to this revelation, the nation of Israel alone was given the promise of inheritance of the land by God. Referring to Genesis 12:1–3, we see this is declared by God to Abram, who later became the patriarch Abraham: "Now the Lord had said unto Abram, Get thee out of thy country, and from thy kindred, and from thy father's house, unto a land that I will show thee. And I will make of thee a great nation, and I will bless thee, and make thy name great; and thou shalt be a blessing: And I will bless them that bless thee, and curse him that curseth thee: and in thee shall all families of the earth be blessed." As the Old Testament progresses, any enemy of the nation of Israel was destroyed to keep the Jewish people pure. There has always been a separation of the Jews and the Gentiles throughout the writings of the prophets. Now as the mystery is being revealed in Paul's epistles, the Gentiles will become fellow heirs to the promises made to Abraham by God so long ago.

The second component of the revealed mystery states that the Gentiles will be part of the same body that is usually referred to in Paul's epistles as the Body of Christ. An example of this is Ephesians 4:12: "For the perfecting of the saints, for the work of the ministry, for the edifying of the body of Christ."

The believers who have put their trust in the Lord Jesus Christ as Savior comprise the body of believers, or specifically the Body of Christ. This body refers to anyone who has become a believer, including Jews, Gentiles, or any other group of people.

The third component of the mystery affirms that the Gentiles are now partakers of God's promise in Christ by the truth of the gospel. Ephesians 2:12–13 explains this by saying, "That at that time ye were without Christ, being aliens from the commonwealth of Israel and strangers from the covenants of promise, having no hope, and without God in the world: But now in Christ Jesus ye who sometimes were afar off are made nigh by the blood of Christ." Continuing with this clarification of the mystery, Paul states the following truth about the Body of Christ in Ephesians 2:14–16: "For he is our peace, who hath made both one, and hath broken down the middle wall of partition between us; Having abolished in his flesh the enmity, even the law of commandments contained in ordinances; for to make in himself of twain one new man, so making peace; and that he might reconcile both unto God in *one body* by the cross, having slain the enmity thereby."

Looking in Matthew 27:51, we see a reference to what the middle wall of partition refers: "And behold the veil of the temple was rent in twain from the top to the bottom; and the earth did quake and the rock rent." The veil that separated the Jews and their Mosaic law from the outsiders, or the Gentiles was torn in two from the top to the bottom; this could have been accomplished only by God and the satisfaction of Jesus Christ dying on the cross for our sins to set us free. Jesus fulfilled the law with His death on the cross, and at this time Paul was defining the spectrum of the mystery related to the truth that Jew and Gentile are now contained in one new man made from two distinct groups of people, referred to as the Body of Christ. In Ephesians 4, Paul is discussing the unity of believers and states in verse 4, "There is one body." Anyone who becomes a believer in the death, burial, and resurrection of the Lord Jesus Christ is ushered into the Body of Christ. There is no law to attempt to follow, no effort of works to accomplish, or no special enlightenment to achieve. How wonderful is our Lord, and how secure and safe we are in the Body of Christ!

It is amazing to contemplate the significance of the mystery. During the Old Testament times, the mystery of the Body of Christ was hidden. The law was given to Moses for the nation of Israel, not to attempt to keep, but to demonstrate the need for a Savior. The apostle Paul explains this in Galatians 3:23–25: "But before faith came, we were kept under the law, shut up unto the faith which should afterwards be revealed. Wherefore the law was our schoolmaster to bring us unto Christ, that we might be justified by faith. But after that faith is come, we are no longer under a schoolmaster." The prophets proclaimed the coming of the Kingdom for the nation of Israel. When the Jews rejected Jesus Christ as their Messiah, the Kingdom was set aside and the Body of Christ was phased in, as can be seen progressively in the book of Acts.

Before his ascension into heaven, Jesus Christ was asked an important transitional question by His apostles. Acts 1:6 states, "When they therefore were come together, they asked of him, saying, Lord, wilt thou at this time restore again the kingdom to Israel?" Jesus's answer to his apostles is very revealing, as seen in Acts 1:7–8: "And he said unto them, It is not for you to know the times or the seasons, which the father hath put in his own power. But ye shall receive power, after that the Holy Ghost is come upon you: and ye shall be witnesses unto me both in Jerusalem and in all Judea, and in Samaria, and to the uttermost parts of the earth." The Kingdom as prophesied in the Old Testament was not going to be set up at this time when Jesus was returning to heaven. We see when the Kingdom is restored to the nation of Israel in of Revelation 20:4: "And I saw thrones and they sat upon them, and judgment was given unto them: and I saw the souls of them that were beheaded for the witness of Jesus and for the word of God, and which had not worshiped the beast, neither his image, neither had received his mark upon their foreheads, or in their hands: and they lived and reigned with Christ for a thousand years."

In Ephesians 3:7 Paul continues to validate his purpose by the gift of God's grace, which is manifested through the power of God. We might wonder where all of this grace and direction for Paul's service to the Lord Jesus Christ began. Again, looking at the progression of phasing out of the Kingdom of the nation of Israel and phasing in of the Body of Christ, we need to return to the book of Acts.

As a persecutor of Christians, Saul is converted to belief when the Lord Jesus appears to him on the road to Damascus. In Acts 9:1 we read, "And Saul, yet breathing out threatenings and slaughter against the disciples of the Lord, went unto the high priest. And desired of him letters to Damascus to the synagogues, that if he found any of this way, whether they were men or women, he might bring them bound unto Jerusalem. And as he journeyed, he came near Damascus: and suddenly there shined round about him a light from heaven: And he fell to the earth, and heard a voice saying unto him, Saul, Saul, why persecutest thou me?"

Then Saul asked what he was to do and was told by Jesus to go into the city and he would be told what to do. None of the men with Saul saw the Lord, but they heard a voice as they were standing. Saul had fallen to the ground by the power of the Lord, but now stood and was led by the men, due to his sudden blindness, to the city of Damascus. Saul continued in blindness and did not eat or drink for three days. A disciple in Damascus named Ananias was given instructions by the Lord as seen in verse 11: "Arise, and go into the street which is called Straight, and inquire in the house of Judas for one called Saul, of Tarsus: for behold he prayeth. And hath seen in a vision a man named Ananias coming in, and putting his hand on him, that he might receive his sight." Ananias told the Lord that he had heard of Saul's persecution of the believers and was concerned about his motives toward the believers. The Lord answered him this way: "Go thy way: for he is a chosen vessel unto me, to bear my name before the Gentiles, and kings, and the children of Israel: For I will show him how great things he must suffer for my name's sake."

This verse proclaims God's purpose for choosing and calling Saul as a believer and the ministry he would have for the Lord, which would focus on carrying the truth of Jesus Christ to the Gentiles and suffering for the name of the Lord Jesus Christ. An interesting observation concerning this Scripture is the order of Saul's ministry presented to Ananias. Saul was to go before the Gentiles, kings, and the children of Israel. Reading the progression of Saul's ministry in the book of Acts, we see the reverse is actually true, since Saul went directly to the children of Israel in the synagogues. Ananias did put his hands on Saul, as the Lord had proclaimed, and said to him beginning in Acts 9:17,

"Brother, Saul the Lord even Jesus, that appeared unto thee in the way as thou camest, hast sent me, that thou mightest receive thy sight, and be filled with the Holy Ghost. And immediately there fell from his eyes as it had been scales: and he received sight forthwith, and arose, and was baptized. And when he had received meat, he was strengthened. Then was Saul certain days with the disciples which were at Damascus. And straightway he preached Christ in the synagogues, that he is the Son of God."

Then Saul, who was first called Paul in Acts 13:9, continued to go to the children of Israel first until Acts 20:24–25: "But none of these things move me, neither count I my life dear unto myself, so that I might finish my course with joy, and the ministry, which I have received of the Lord Jesus, to testify the gospel of the grace of God. And now, behold, I know that ye all among whom I have gone preaching the kingdom of God shall see my face no more." Paul is turning away from the children of Israel and beginning the portion of the ministry God called him to complete as we saw in Acts 9:15. This is Paul's main calling to preach to the Gentiles the mystery as it was revealed to Paul at this time, after being hidden in God from the beginning of the world.

Returning to Ephesians 3:8, we see that Paul is humbled that God would give to him the honor to preach to the Gentiles the "unsearchable riches" of Christ, and most importantly, in verse 9 to "make all men see what is the fellowship of the mystery, which from the beginning of the world hath been hid in God who created all things by Jesus Christ." The word "fellowship" in the Greek is *koinonia*. The actual meaning is "partnership or participation of the Saints in the Body of Christ." This is an entirely new entity in God's progressive revelation as the Bible unfolds from Genesis to Revelation. Since the mystery as revealed to Paul has been hidden from the beginning of the world, we know that there are no prophecies or indicators of the mystery anywhere prior to Paul's proclamation in the Word of God.

In Ephesians 3:10–11, we see God's intent for the mystery to be revealed at this point in time: "To the intent that now unto the principalities and powers in heavenly places might be known by the church the manifold wisdom of God. According to the eternal purpose which he purposed in Christ Jesus our Lord." God, in His great sovereign wisdom, had determined to reveal the mystery at this time, which was His eternal plan from the beginning of time. We can derive comfort from this truth in God's Word that we continue to live in this era of grace as members of the Body of Christ. We clearly see the long-suffering of God in our present time to withhold immediate judgment for sin and disobedience that was prevalent in the Old Testament narrative when the penalty for sin was exacted as the law was transgressed.

Justification

All of this truth regarding the mystery and God's imparting of His divine grace is purposed in Christ Jesus our Lord, who paid the ultimate penalty for our sin. The Greek word for "justification" is *dikaioo*, which means "to render innocent." Verbs that end in "oo" generally mean to bring out that which a person is, or that which is desired. *Dikaioo* means to bring out the fact that a person is righteous, or if he is not, to make him righteous. In the New Testament, *dikaioo* never means to make someone righteous by doing away with his violation of the law by himself bearing the condemnation of the imposed sentence. Man, in his fallen condition, can never do anything to pay for his own sinfulness and be liberated from the sentence of guilt that is upon him. In our legal system, when a guilty person has paid the penalty for his crime, he is free from the condemnation of the law. In the New Testament, *dikaioo* in the active tense means "to recognize, to set forth as righteous, to justify." Paul states in 1 Timothy 3:16 that God/Jesus Christ was "justified in the Spirit" or made righteous not by the law. His high claims of being the Son of God, the Messiah, and the Redeemer were justified or proved true by the descent of the Holy Spirit upon Him at His baptism, resulting in the miracles that He performed, the life that He lived, and finally through His resurrection from the dead.

The New Testament records how being justified by God and declared just before Him are achieved in the lives of men. We are justified before God by Christ through grace. When one receives Christ, he recognizes God's right over his life. His justification simultaneously performs a miracle in him and changes his character. He does not obey God because he is afraid of the consequences of his disobedience, but because of the grace that is imputed to him *in Christ*, which changed his character and made him just. These truths are supported in Romans 3:24, which states, "Being justified freely by his grace through the redemption that is in Christ Jesus."

Two important components of justification include the understanding of propitiation and the blood of Christ. Looking at Romans 3:25, we read, "Whom God hath set forth to be a propitiation through faith in his blood, to declare his righteousness for the remission of sins that are past, through the forbearance of God." Of course the blood refers to Jesus as stated in the previously cited verse of Romans 3:24.

In order to understand the implication of these two verses regarding justification, we must first go to Hebrews 9:4–5 to discuss the mercy seat, "which had the golden censer, and the ark of the covenant overlaid round about with gold, wherein was the golden pot, that had manna, and Aaron's rod that budded, and the tables of the covenant. And over it the cherubims of glory shadowing the mercy seat; of which we cannot now speak particularly." The lid or covering of the ark of the covenant was made of pure gold. On or before the ark, the high priest sprinkled the blood of the expiratory animal sacrifices on the yearly great Day of Atonement when the sins of the nation of Israel were covered. The apostle Paul, by applying this name of propitiation to Christ in Romans 3:25, asserts that Christ was the true mercy seat, the antitype of the cover of the ark of the covenant. Jesus Christ is designated as the mercy seat, because He is not only the place where the sinner deposits his sins, but He himself is the means of expiation, which describes the satisfaction or atonement before a holy God. Jesus is not like the priest in the Old Testament whose expiation of the people is accomplished through the blood of another and not his own. This truth is supported in Hebrews 9:24–25: "For Christ is not entered into the holy places made with hands, which are the figures of the true; but into heaven itself, now to appear in the presence of God for us. Nor yet that he should offer himself often, as the high priest entereth into the holy place every year with blood of others;"

The second component of justification relates to the blood. The Greek word for "blood" as used in Romans 3:25 is *haima*, denoting the atoning blood of Christ. This use of the word "blood" designates the life of Christ offered for an atonement contrasted with the blood of beasts slain in sacrifice. The Bible makes this contrast clear in Hebrews 9:12: "Neither by the blood of goats and calves, but by his own blood he entered in once into the holy place, having obtained eternal redemption for us." The blood of Christ, therefore, represents the title that He gave for our atonement.

When referring to the blood of Christ, we see a definite progression. The blood was shed at one point in time on the cross at Calvary, but the references to the blood are applied differently to the nation of Israel during the life of Christ and then to the Body of Christ as revealed by the apostle Paul at that exact point on God's timeline.

For example, in Matthew 26:28 Jesus states, "For this is my blood that of the new covenant which for many is poured out for remission of sins." In Mark 14:24 Jesus says, "This is my blood that of the new covenant which for many is poured out." Then again in Luke 22:20, Jesus says, "In like manner also the cup after having supped saying, this cup the new covenant in my blood which for you is poured out." We see clearly that the new covenant is for the house of Israel. Look at Jeremiah 31:31, which states, "Behold, the days come, saith the Lord, that I will make a new covenant with the house of Israel, and with the house of Judah."

For clarification of the new covenant in Christ for the nation of Israel, we begin reading in Hebrews 8:7:

> For if that first covenant had been faultless, then should no place have been sought for the second. For finding fault with them, he saith, BEHOLD, THE DAYS COME SAITH THE LORD, WHEN I WILL MAKE A NEW COVENANT WITH THE HOUSE OF ISRAEL AND WITH THE HOUSE OF JUDAH. NOT ACCORDING TO THE COVENANT THAT I MADE WITH THEIR FATHERS, IN THE DAY WHEN I TOOK THEM BY THE HAND TO LEAD THEM OUT OF THE LAND OF EGYPT, BECAUSE THEY CONTINUED NOT IN MY COVENANT, AND I REGARDED THEM NOT, SAITH THE LORD.

Now turning to the apostle Paul's description of the blood of Christ in one of his epistles that also refers to the Body of Christ to whom his teaching is addressed, we read in Colossians 1:14, "In whom we have redemption, through his blood, even the forgiveness of sins."

Justification is the acceptance by God of the finished work of Jesus Christ on the cross for the remission of our sins. Through this act of justification, we are able to be restored to a relationship of fellowship with God through Jesus Christ. We don't need to go through another human being to have access to God. This is freedom and liberty, not to live any way we want, but to serve the Lord in the way He has called us.

Heresy in the Church and the Believer's Position in Christ

Now that we have reviewed the divine process for our arrival at the point of being *in Christ*, we need to continue in our progressive study of God's Word by examining the Scriptures from the heading of this chapter. Colossians 2:9–10 states, "For in him dwelleth all the fullness of the Godhead bodily. And ye are complete in him, which is the head of all principality and power."

Since the theme of Colossians is polemic in presentation, Paul is citing these two Sriptures to counteract the preceding scripture referring to false teaching prevalent in the world at the time of the writing of the book of Colossians. Colossians 2:8 states, "Beware lest any man spoil you through philosophy and vain deceit, after the tradition of men, after the rudiments of the world, and not after Christ."

To understand our secure position in Christ, examination of the meaning of verse 8 is crucial at this point. Taking each important word of the verse, defining the word, and summarizing the entire verse will enrich the meaning of Colossians 2:9–10 related to our relationship with the Lord Jesus Christ.

<u>Greek word/English meaning</u>

1. *Blepo*/beware: to look at, behold, beware, to beware as a warning[*]
2. *Me*/lest: to expresses an absolute denial of what is to follow

---

[*] The verb beware is in the present imperative active, which may indicate a command to do something in the future involving continuous or repeated action. The subject is acting some way upon himself or concerning himself. This word as used by Paul alerts us to pay attention to the warning that follows.

3. *Tis*/man: referring to any person and not specific of gender
4. *Sulagogeo*/spoil: to lead away as booty, seduce, make prey of[†]
5. *Dia*/through: Represents a channel of the act
6. *Philosophia*/philosophy: Jewish sophistry or wisdom (used only here in NT)
7. *Kai*/and: cumulative effect in sentence structure
8. *Kenos*/vain: empty[‡]
9. *Apate*/deceit: refers to delusion and deceivableness
10. *Kata*/after: according to
11. *Paradosis*/tradition: a precept or the Jewish traditionary law
12. *Stoicheion*/rudiments: something orderly in arrangement or fundamental[§]

In summary, Colossians 2:8 is a continuous warning for the church at Colossae and to the Body of Christ today: be aware of potentially harmful influences of false teaching by men in the world, but rather follow after the truth of who we are *in Christ*.

The actual heresy contained within Colossians 2:8 needs to be studied in detail, but for the purposes of comparison to our relationship with Jesus Christ, a brief exposition will be made. The Greek word *haireses* means "heresy" and is delineated into three meanings:

I. A chosen course of thought and action—one's chosen opinion, tenet, a sect party, such as the Sadducees, the Pharisees, and the Christians.

The Sadducees (*Saddoukaios*) were a member of one of the religious parties that existed among the Jews in the days of our Lord. They were named from a certain Zadok, a disciple of Antiogonus of Socho mentioned in the

---

[†] The word *sulagogogeo* is only used here in the Scriptures. The present active participle tense denotes continuous or repeated action that is contemporaneous with the leading verb, whether that action occurs in the past, present, or future.

[‡] The word *kenos* indicates the hollowness of something or somebody and is unaccompanied by the demonstration of the Holy Spirit and power.

[§] The apostle Paul calls the ceremonial ordinances of the Mosaic law the element of the world, or worldly elements. In Galatians 4:9 he states, "But now, after that ye have known God, or rather are known of God, how turn ye again to the weak and beggarly elements, whereunto ye desire again to be in bondage?" These weak and beggarly elements are considered in opposition to a relationship with Christ as Colossians 2:8 embodies.

Mishna (the first part of the Talmud, containing traditional oral interpretations of scriptural ordinances, compiled by the rabbis about AD 200) as having received the oral law from Simon the Just.

The Pharisees (*perisha*—separated) were called Separatists by their adversaries, which was probably derived at the time of Zerubbabel and Ezra when Israel separated from the heathen dwelling in the land and from their uncleanness. This is substantiated in Ezra 6:21: "And the children of Israel, which were come again out of captivity, and all such as had separated themselves unto them from the filthiness of the heathen of the land, to seek the LORD God of Israel, did eat." Their exclusiveness was reflected in the small number of about six thousand. They were stricter than most of Israel in their view of uncleanness. Following the captivity, the priests and scribes continued to separate until the Maccabean period, when two distinct opposing parties developed. The Sadducean party came from the priests and the Pharisees from the scribes.

The Christians (*Christianos*—follower of Christ) were first called Christians at Antioch according to Acts 11:26: "And the disciples were called Christians first in Antioch." This word is also used only in Acts 26:28, "Then Agrippa said unto Paul, Almost thou persuadest me to be a Christian," and in 1 Peter 4:16, "Yet if any man suffer as a Christian, let him not be ashamed; but let him glorify God on this behalf."

Refer to chart 7 in the appendix: "Comparison of Sadducees and Pharisees." The differences between these two sects are very clear. The Sadducees were steeped in ceremony and strict adherence to the law, with man's abilities and freedoms directing the temporal life. The Pharisees were very rigid and unyielding, with belief in the supernatural and an afterlife and a human element of cooperation with God.

To further explain point 5 under the Sadducees column, the event of a priest burning a new heifer, the significance of this ordinance for the entire nation was to ensure that special precautions for preparation were observed to safeguard the purity of the priest who was burning the heifer. Some of these precautions resulted from the disagreements between the sages of Israel and the Sadducees. The preparation of the red heifer was a prominent point of disagreement. Since the Sadducees did not adhere to the Mosaic tradition and its interpretation of Scripture, they believed that purity produced by one priest sprinkling water on another was not sufficient and the officiating priest had to be immersed in water and wait an entire day until after sunset to be considered cleansed. The Sadducees were actually undermining the authority of the Sinai revelation to Moses by creating *their own rules, such as this example of purification, which were not supported in the word of God.*[1]

Point 7 under Sadducees, denying the existence of angel or spirit, originated from their regard of angels of the Old Testament as transitory, insubstantial representations of Jehovah. They disbelieved the angelical system that was developed among the Jews after the captivity.

Under point 8 for the importance of human freedom, the belief was that man was placed at his own disposal. The Sadducees rejected the thought that a divine cooperation took place in human actions. They denied all absolute preordination and made man's choice of evil or good to depend entirely on the exercise of free will and self-determination.

Let's examine chart 8 in the appendix: "Comparison of Pharisees and Christians." In point 1, we see that the Pharisees strongly believed that the moral precepts of the law were to elevate men, and they strictly adhered to these moral precepts. In contrast the Christians believed that Jesus Christ came to fulfill the law and was a "schoolmaster to bring us to himself that we might be justified by faith." Further reading in Galatians 3:24–25 will be beneficial for clarification of this contrast.

Point 2 compares the detailed law and its minutia with the life of grace and the fruit that fulfills above and beyond what the law was able to do. Read Matthew 12:1–13 and Galatians 5:18–22 for details of this point of comparison.

For point 3 we compare the most solemn truths that were handled as mere matters of curious speculation or means to entrap an adversary with the true faith that is not external, but a fruit of the inner man. Read Matthew 22:35 and Ephesians 5:9.

In point 4 we see that the Pharisees usually desired to attract attention and the admiration of men, compared to the Christians who bear humility as a fruit that is brought forth as the Christian beholds the truth of God's glory. Read Matthew 6:2 and 2 Corinthians 3:18.

Finally, in point 5 we compare the shunning of the poor classes of society with compassion for the poor since all have sinned. Read Luke 7:39 and Romans 3:23.

II. The second meaning for "heresies" involves dissensions arising from diversity of opinions and aims. In Galatians 5:20 we read, "Idolatry, witchcraft, hatred, variance, emulations, wrath, strife, seditions, heresies." These are called the "works of the flesh" and are practiced as a lifestyle by those who are not walking in the truth of the Spirit. 1 Corinthians 11:19 refers to the people misusing the Lord's supper, "For there must be also heresies among you, that they which are approved may be made manifest among you."

III. The meaning of "heresies" directly related to "rightly dividing the word of truth" involves doctrinal departures from revealed truth, or erroneous views. Scriptures describing this heresy include Titus 3:10–11, "A man that is an heretic after the first and second admonition reject, Knowing that he that is such is subverted, and sinneth, being condemned of himself"; 2 Peter 2:1, "But there were false prophets also among the people, even as there shall be false teachers among you, who privily shall bring in damnable heresies, even denying the Lord that bought them, and bring upon themselves swift destruction"; and Acts 20:29–30, "For I know this that after my departing shall grievous wolves enter in among you, not sparing the flock. Also of your own selves shall men arise, speaking perverse things, to draw away disciples after them." These scriptures are informative regarding the importance of studying God's Word to behold the truth of who we are in Christ.

Now that some of the heresies encountered at the time of Paul's writing of the book of Colossians have been examined, we need to return to the Scriptures that were written to counteract these heresies. Colossians 2:9–10: "For in him dwelleth all the fullness of the Godhead bodily. And ye are complete in him, which is the head of all principality and power."

We will unpack these Scriptures and explore some of the wonderful truths that are contained within Paul's writings.

In Colossians 2:9, the preposition "for" is very important as a transitional word from verse 8, which described being deceived by man's philosophy and not walking in the truth of Jesus Christ. "For" provides a bridge to Colossians 9, the reason not to be deceived by false teaching.

The Greek word *katoikeo* means "dwelleth" or "to house permanently or to reside." The actual meaning within the context of this verse is "to dwell as the fullness of the Godhead in Christ." The verb tense is present indicative active, which asserts something that is occurring while the speaker is making the statement.

The word "fullness" is *pleroma* in the Greek, which means completion, copiousness, multitude, what is filled, as a container.

The word "Godhead" is *theotes* and is only used in Colossians 2:9 in the New Testament. The meaning of *theotes* is "Godhead as directly revealed or God's personality" as distinguished from the Greek word *theiotes*, translated "Godhead," used in Romans 1:20, which means "divinity or divine power and majesty, a concept arrived at by observing God's might works."

The word "bodily" is *somatikos* in the Greek and means "corporeally or physically." The verb tense used here is an adverb which qualifies the meaning of a verb by indicating the time, place, or manner in which its action is accomplished. The word *somatikos* is used only in this verse in the New Testament.

When the words and meanings are examined and summarized, we can see that some heresies of Paul's day may exist today with different names attached. We need to look to the Lord Jesus Christ for truth because in Him is permanently housed the completion of the total personality of God. From regarding a plethora of other supporting scriptures, we never see the word "trinity," but we know that the Godhead refers to the essence of God contained in the Father, Son, and the Holy Spirit. Within the Godhead each person is unique, but essential to the manifestation of equality.

The Godhead needs to be examined further to facilitate our understanding of Colossian 2:9. When we consider the spectrum of components concerning the Godhead, we can identify five that will help clarify the context of this verse. To further your study, you are encouraged to read these Scriptures and compare them with any others you may find.

I. The Deity of Christ as He is equal to God the Father with supportive Scriptures.

    A. Colossians 1:15–19. These Scriptures combat the false teaching in Colossae that Jesus Christ was not God.

    B. John1:1–15. These Scriptures are written to prove Christ's deity to lead men to salvation.

    C. Hebrews 1:1–4. These Scriptures show that Christ because He was God did a work that was superior to the teaching of Judaism, especially the sacrifices of animals.

    D. Philippians 2:5–11. These Scriptures demonstrate the ultimate sacrifice of God as He took on the form of a servant to encourage bond servants in their ministries, as they meditate on this truth and realize that nothing is beneath them to do in their service for Christ.

II. The mind of Christ, which is in the believer. Philippians 2:3–5.

    A. He esteemed (lead in the mind) others greater than Himself.

    B. He esteemed us greater than His glory and His comfort that He had with the Godhead, the joy of His relationship with them.

    C. His scope was not His own position, comfort, and glory.

    D. Christ did not look on His own things, but gave with love and heartbreak on the things of others. *His own things*: throne, crown, position, name. *Things He saw as He looked to others*: sin, sorrow, desperation, need. He laid aside His rights to retain His position by exchanging His throne for a stable and His crown for a cross.

III. Form. Essence/expression; identical to essence, emphasis on expression.

There is no human counterpart to adequately explain this concept, and any illustration would only fall short. Looking at the Lord, Jesus always has been and never will cease to be deity. This is His essence. Prior to His incarnation, He was fully displaying everything, taking all rights and privileges as God. He had the right to be worshiped and served, clothed with all the divine splendor that made Him and the other two members of the Godhead unapproachable. After the fall in the Garden of Eden, sinful man was not capable of worshiping or serving anything other than himself. Had Jesus held on to His manifestation as God, man would have been eternally lost. A sinless offering of a human had to be given. As we read in Hebrews 10:4, "It is not possible that the blood of bulls and of goats should take away sins." Only the sinless God/man Jesus Christ could be the Savior of humanity.

IV. God/Man. God had to add to Himself humanity to be the Savior of the world, so He became the God/Man.

Any one of the three persons of the Godhead could have performed this act. The Bible stated in 1 John 4:14, "that the Father sent the Son to be the Savior of the World." Jesus demonstrated His essential deity in John 10:18, describing the greatest power is to raise the dead. We also see this in Ephesians 1:19–23 regarding the power of God to raise Jesus Christ from the dead. In Acts 20:28, the church of God is referenced, "which He has purchased with His own blood." If He became less than deity, then His blood would have been insufficient. In 1 Timothy 3:16 "God is manifested in the flesh," not in full expression, but in essence. 1 Corinthians 2:7–8 states, "But we speak the wisdom of God in a mystery, even the hidden wisdom, which God ordained before the world unto our glory: Which none of the princes of this world knew: for had they known it, they would not have crucified the Lord of glory." God gave up His right to outward expression and outward manifestation of His deity. Jesus was always conscious of being God. He gave up His manifestation by adding a new form of expression He had not had before, which was that of a servant. This concept involves limiting by adding, or subtraction by adding.

V. Trinity. "Trinity" is a term not found in the Bible, but originated by man to explain the Godhead.

> God the Father, God the Son, and God the Holy Spirit (John 14:26, Ephesians 1:3–13) have always existed and will always exist. God the Son was manifested in the flesh, with the complete essence of God to be the propitiation for our sins (Romans 3:24–25) and take on the form of a servant. We are being conformed to the image of Christ (Romans 8:29-30; Romans 12:2; 2 Corinthians 3;18; and Colossians 1:6) and as bond servants (Romans 6:18 and 2 Timothy 2:24–26) we will manifest the humility that Christ did while He was on the earth (Philippians 2:4).
>
> Moving ahead to Colossians 2:10, "And ye are complete in him, which is the head of all principality and power," we need to examine the meaning of the pertinent words and grammatical tenses.
>
> While verse 9 was describing the fullness of the deity of the Lord Jesus Christ, verse 10 goes on to describe the position of the believer in Christ.

Greek word/English meaning

1. *Kai*/and: makes the connection with verse nine as "a cumulative force."
2. *Este*/are: are.**¶
3. *Pleroo*/complete: to make replete, to cram a net, level up a hollow. Nothing else can be added.††**

** This verb is used in the present indicative active tense and occurs only in the active and middle voices in the New Testament. The active voice may indicate a command to do something in the future that involves continuous or repeated action as accomplished by the subject.

†† *These definitions are very apropos to the understanding of the word "complete." When a fisherman throws out a net and trolls along in the water, he will pull in the net to determine how many fish were trapped. Often the catch is very full, but imagine not being able to fit one more fish in the net. Or when filling up a hole so smoothly that there is no indentation. This is the meaning of being complete in the Lord Jesus Christ. We have everything, and there is nothing that can be added to make our salvation more complete. Actually, if a person attempts to add anything to the finished work of Jesus Christ, it is considered ineffectual works. The Bible is clear that our works do not contribute in any way to what Jesus Christ accomplished on the cross. Read Titus 3:5 and Ephesians 2:4–9 for a greater understanding of this truth.

4. *Kephale*/head: seizing the head; Christ is the head of the Body of Christ and all principality and power.
5. *Arche*/principality: commencement, beginning, rule authority, domain.
6. *Exousia*/power: privilege, mastery, superhuman, dominion, government.

In summary of Colossians 2:10, we can conclude that *in Christ* we have everything, can add nothing to what He has already accomplished, and Christ has authority over everything which exists.

We have examined Colossians 2:9–10, which helps elucidate our position of being *in Christ*, relating the Lord Jesus Christ and His deity to His body of believers and the eternal completeness of our relationship with Him.

Let's look now at the blessings we have as believers in the Lord Jesus Christ. The gift of salvation is free for us, but Jesus had to die on the cross for this freedom to be obtained. We have examined this truth of the cross several times in this book related to the gospel, salvation, justification, and sanctification.

Now we want to see the manifestation of this glorious relationship in our lives and how all of these truths relate to the stages of spiritual growth of the believer.

In Ephesians 1:3–14, the apostle Paul lists several blessings given to us who are members of the Body of Christ. To behold the significance of these blessings, you will need to take sufficient time to examine each verse and cross-reference them in Paul's other epistles.

Spiritual Blessings from God the Father of Our Lord Jesus Christ

1. We have all spiritual blessings in heavenly places *in Christ*. (1:3)
2. He has chosen us *in Him* before the foundation of the world. (1:4)
3. He has predestinated us unto the adoption of children by Jesus Christ to himself, according to the good pleasure of His will. (1:5)
4. He has made us accepted in the beloved. (1:6)
5. We have redemption through His blood and the forgiveness of sins. (1:7)
6. He has given us all wisdom and understanding. (1:8)
7. He has made known to us the mystery of His will. (1:9)

8. In the dispensation of the fullness of times, He might gather together in one all things *in Christ* on earth and in heaven *in Him*. (1:10)
9. *In Christ* we have an inheritance being predestinated according to His purpose Who works all things according to His will. (1:11)
10. We should be to the praise of His glory, who first trusted *in Christ*. (1:12)
11. We are sealed with the Holy Spirit of promise. (1:13)
12. The Holy Spirit is the earnest of our inheritance until we are glorified through ultimate sanctification. (1:14)

Through these spiritual blessings, believers at every level of spiritual growth are secure *in Christ* and will be transformed and renewed by the working of the Holy Spirit in our lives, bringing us into all truth. As we mature and transition through each of the four stages of Christian growth, we become increasingly conformed to the image of our Lord and Savior Jesus Christ.

Now might be a good time to review charts 4 and 1 in the appendix for the four growth stages of a believer and how our transformation occurs as illuminated in 2 Corinthians 3:18, as we are renewed by the work of the Holy Spirit and not by our own effort. In chapter 7, 2 Corinthians 3:18, as well as other Scriptures reflecting the believer's spiritual transformation, will be examined related to the progressive sanctification process. Looking in chapter 5 for any specifics of each growth stage will assist in making the connection between how we grow *in Christ*, becoming progressively more like Him as we journey in this life toward our final destination in heaven when we will reach our ultimate sanctification.

Also, at this juncture, you might want to review the characteristics of our two Christian women, Alice Buffington and Heather Cook, in chapter 2. The connection between these two women as described in chapter 2 and the expansion of information in the subsequent chapters should be apparent at this point.

Do you remember the prayer at the beginning of this chapter to change your thinking from being a sinner saved by grace to a saint saved by grace who is still capable of sinning? Does this perspective resonate in your heart at this point? To further your thinking in this direction, look at the greetings of Paul's epistles that are directed to multiple persons at the time when the mystery was revealed: Ephesians 1:1, "Paul an apostle of Jesus Christ by the will of God, to the *saints* which are at Ephesus, and to the faithful in Christ Jesus"; Philippians 1:1, "Paul and Timothy, the servants of Jesus Christ, to all the *saints* in Christ Jesus which are at Philippi, with the bishops and deacons"; and Colossians 1:2, "To the *saints* and faithful brethren in Christ which are at Colossae." Paul does not address the "sinners" at Ephesus, Philippi, and Colossae; he calls them *saints*. Is that because they are striving to do well as Christians, are superior to others, or have some enlightenment that no one else has? No, it's due completely to the finished work of the Lord Jesus Christ on the cross.

To further expound upon the significance of the cross, we turn to Colossians 1:20: "And, having made peace through the blood of his cross, by him to reconcile all things unto himself; by him, I say, whether they be things in earth, or things in heaven." The section of the verse regarding peace and the cross becomes more understandable when observed closely.

The word "peace" is *eirenopoieo* in the Greek and means "to put an end to strife." The verb tense is aorist participle active, which is simple action accomplished by the subject of the verb.

The word "through" is *dia* in the Greek and means a channel of an act.

The word "blood" is *haima* in the Greek and means the atoning blood of Christ, representing the life He gave for our atonement.

Looking at the word "cross," which is *stauros* in the Greek, we can see the depth of meaning in the act of our Lord Jesus Christ as He gave His life for us. The definition of "cross" is "a stake or post as set upright, a pole or cross as an instrument of capital punishment, the atonement of Christ, and an instrument of torture that was not abolished until the time of Constantine in the fourth century, the first Roman emperor who claimed to be a Christian." Crucifixion was at the same time an execution, a pillory (stocks), and an instrument of torture. In the New Testament, *stauros* means

1. A Roman cross consisting of a straight piece of wood fixed in the earth with a transverse beam fastened across its top to which the person's hands were nailed. This is the type of cross on which the Lord Jesus suffered. Mark 15:25: "And it was the third hour, and they crucified him."

2. The whole passion of Christ and the merit of His suffering and death; Ephesians 2:16: "And that he might reconcile both unto God in one body by the cross, having slain the enmity thereby." The doctrine of merit; 1 Corinthians 1:17: "For Christ sent me not to baptize, but to preach the gospel."

3. That portion of affliction which is endured by pious and good men as a trial of their faith, to conform to the example of their crucified master. Matthew 10:38: "And he that taketh not his cross, and followeth after me, is not worth of me." The expressions of taking up or carrying the cross allude to the Roman custom of making the criminal carry the cross on which he was to suffer; John 19:17: "And he bearing his cross went forth into a place called the place of a skull, which is called in the Hebrew Golgotha."

Anytime we may hear or read of the antagonism to the cross of Christ, we must understand it as antagonism to a redemption that was accomplished through the deepest humiliation, not through a display of power and glory. Philippians 2:5–8: "Let this mind be in you, which was also in Christ Jesus: Who, being in the form of God, thought it not robbery to be equal with God. But made himself of no reputation, and took upon him the form of a servant, and was made in the likeness of men: And being found in fashion as a man, he humbled himself, and became obedient unto death, even the death on the cross."

It is not often the sacrifice of Christ that is emphasized in the New Testament, but the blood of Christ as a means of redemption. This is because the blood refers to the sacrifice, while the cross refers more to the shame. To the Christian, the relationship we have with the Lord Jesus Christ through the atoning blood puts an end to the strife and bondage of sin, and this redemption is obtained only by the suffering of our Lord on the cross.

In summary of chapter 6, we as believers have been saved by the death, burial, and resurrection of the Lord Jesus Christ. We have been placed *in Christ* as a member of the Body of Christ, the mystery which was hidden from the foundation of the world until its revelation by the apostle Paul, whose ministry was directed to the Gentiles. As believers who are complete *in Christ*, we have bestowed on us all of the spiritual blessings, as we grow through transformation by the Holy Spirit's renewal from glory to glory.

Questions for Group Discussion or Individual Study

1. Explain in your own words the scope of the gospel as described at the beginning of this chapter. Why are the number of witnesses to the resurrection important? Why did the Jewish leaders try to deny the resurrection by paying Roman soldiers to steal the body of Jesus from the tomb?

2. Why does Paul refer to "my gospel"? Does this differ from other references to the gospel in God's Word? Why or why not?

3. Read Colossians 2:9–10 again. Define what the Godhead is and how it relates to the Lord Jesus Christ. Are you able to do anything to save yourself? Is there anything you can add to what Jesus Christ has accomplished? Provide additional Scriptures to support your answer.

4. Do you know anyone who believes that the disciples went into the tomb and stole the body of Jesus, thereby proving that the resurrection did not occur? Have you ever wondered if that may have happened? How can you defend the resurrection to those who do not believe?

5. The mystery as delineated in Ephesians 3 was described as being revealed now or at the present time when the epistle was written. Is this the only mystery implied in God's Word? Are you able to find any other mysteries? The Greek word *musterion* refers to something that is hidden but will be revealed at the time God has ordained. Why do you think this mystery described by the apostle Paul was revealed at this time in God's eternal plan? Why did the apostle Paul reveal the mystery, and not Peter, or John?

6. Two distinct groups have been examined in chapter 6: the nation of Israel and the Body of Christ. Did God provide two different means of salvation? Why or why not? Are you able to provide Scriptures to support your answer?

7. Compare the ministry of the apostle Peter to the ministry of the apostle Paul. How are they similar? How are they different? Why is Peter called "the apostle to the circumcision"? Why is Paul called "the apostle to the uncircumcision"?

8. Take some time now to examine chart 6 in the appendix. In your Bible study time as you are "rightly dividing" the Word of God, reflect upon the depth of each book and to whom it is directed related to the spiritual growth stage of a Christian.

9. Do you consider yourself a sinner saved by grace or a saint saved by grace who is still capable of sinning? As you answer this question, remember the cost to our Lord Jesus Christ as He was crucified for our sins and became a satisfactory propitiation through His shed blood.

10. Refer to chart 9. Take your Bible, a notebook, and a concordance, and look up the scriptures in each one of these books that talk about being *in Christ*. Ask yourself, "Who am I *in Christ*?". Also, many Scriptures say *in Him* rather than *in Christ*. To get you started, for example, in Romans 3:24 we have redemption *in Christ*. In Romans 8:1 we see there is no condemnation *in Christ Jesus* for those who "walk not after the flesh, but after the Spirit." There are many other Scriptures to find in the epistles of Paul listed in chart 9. When you write them down, take time over the next few months and study the truths you are discovering. You will find great transformation in your spiritual walk as you study and are able to share what you are learning with others.

7

What Does All This Mean to You?

I therefore, the prisoner of the Lord, beseech you that ye walk worthy of the vocation wherewith ye are called.

—EPHESIANS 4:1

That ye might walk worthy of the Lord unto all pleasing, being fruitful in every good work, and increasing in the knowledge of God.

—COLOSSIANS 1:10

What is the most important goal for a pastor or anyone serving in a teaching ministry for the Lord? The simple answer is to feed the sheep. Peter was asked three questions by the Lord Jesus Christ that I believe were for restoration to the ministry after he had denied the Lord three times. In John 21:15–18 we read,

> So when they had dined, Jesus saith to Simon Peter, Simon, son of Jonah, lovest thou me more than these? He saith unto him, Yea, Lord: thou knowest that I love thee. He saith unto him, Feed my lambs. He saith to him again the second time, Simon, son of Jonah, lovest thou me? He saith unto him, Yea, Lord; thou knowest that I love thee. He saith unto him, Feed my sheep. He saith unto him the third time, Simon, son of Jonah, lovest thou me? Peter was grieved because he said unto him the third time, Lovest thou me? And he said unto him, Lord, thou knowest all things; thou knowest that I love thee. Jesus saith unto him, Feed my sheep. Verily, verily, I say unto thee, When thou wast young, thou girdedst thyself, and walkedst whither thou wouldest: but when thou shalt be old, thou shalt stretch forth thy hands, and another shall gird thee, and carry thee whither thou wouldest not.

The Lord provided Peter with three separate commands to continue his ministry based on love to express forgiveness for the three separate denials that Peter uttered when the Lord was arrested and taken before the high priest. Then the Lord contrasted Peter's early service to Himself, manifested as boldness and abruptness without wisdom and discernment, to Peter's eventual death in his old age of wisdom and maturity, which would be crucifixion.

Today in the Body of Christ, often more emphasis is placed upon programs, church attendance, evangelism, or even fellowship. While each one of these components may be a fruit of the believer's walk with the Lord, the paramount reason to attend a local church is to be fed as a sheep by the Word of God. As the pastor is feeding the sheep, the gospel is woven into the teaching, and the fruit of the Spirit will become evident in the body of believers and bring glory and honor to God. Anyone attending the church who may not know the Lord personally will hear the truth of how to become a believer.

Shortly before he was beheaded, Paul passed the baton of ministry to Timothy and exhorted the young pastor and shepherd of the church in 2 Timothy 4:1–5, "I charge thee therefore before God, and the Lord Jesus Christ, who shall judge the quick and the dead at his appearing and his kingdom; Preach the word; be instant in season, out of season; reprove, rebuke, exhort with all longsuffering and doctrine. For the time will come when they will not endure sound doctrine; but after their own lusts shall they heap to themselves teachers, having itching ears; And they shall turn away their ears from the truth, and shall be turned unto fables." These verses clearly and succinctly encourage Timothy to teach the truth of God's Word to his congregants. Paul obviously trusted in Timothy as a pastor who would "rightly divide" the Word of truth and was encouraging him to continue doing what he was already doing, especially as the time of apostasy was drawing near.

Your question at this time might be "Well, that is good for a pastor of a church or for someone in ministry outreach, but how does that apply to me?" And that is a valid question to ask. Now that the areas of Christian growth and our position of who we are *in Christ* have been explored, we need to examine how these truths relate to our individual calling by the Lord.

As we have previously examined the transformed life of a Christian by the Holy Spirit in prior chapters related to progressive sanctification and the four stages of Christian growth, several Scriptures are paramount. In order to truly behold the changes that occur in a believer, we must examine how we are changed. We do not set our minds to becoming more like Jesus Christ through effort of exercising love, faith, self-control, or any other fruit of the Spirit. Conversely, the emerging Christian is beholding the truths in God's Word from the moment of conversion. We read in Colossians 1:5–6, "For the hope which is laid up for you in heaven, whereof ye heard before in the word of the truth of the gospel: Which is come unto you, as it is in all the world; and bringeth forth fruit, as it doth also in you, since the day ye heard of it, and knew the grace of God in truth." When a person hears the gospel, has his eyes opened by the Lord, is given the faith to believe by grace, and turns from a life of sin, the fruit of the Spirit begins to grow at that very moment. A thorough examination of each of these components has been presented in the six previous chapters. The purpose of this chapter is to assist the reader in spiritual comprehension of the transformed life through further observation and illustration, and to understand the effect in an individual's worthy walk with the Lord.

We discussed the root/fruit principle in chapter 5 as presented by the apostle Paul in his epistles, and we examined the tree with an outline of a Bible embedded in its roots. Refer again to chart 5 in the appendix, "Union with Christ as a Small Seed," to see the example of the book of Romans 1–11, which represents the doctrines of the faith, or the root and Romans 12–16, which refers to the manifestation of growth or the fruit in the believer. This current chapter will encompass the progressive sanctification or growth of the believer as observed in his life by the outward fruit that is evidenced.

A Scripture that is essential to the understanding of our ongoing transformation as a "new creature" *in Christ* is 2 Corinthians 3:18, which states, "But we all with open face beholding in a glass the glory of the Lord are changed from glory to glory even as by the spirit of the Lord." Chart 1 in the appendix, "Summary of Verse Analysis on 2 Corinthians 3:18," is used to further elucidate this truth about how we are renewed in our walk with the Lord.

But We

Let's examine each grouping of the verse and expand the meaning for clarification and application. Beginning with "But we," we are seeing a contrast with the presence of the conjunction "but." This conjunction is directing our attention to the preceding verses of 2 Corinthians 3:13–17, which state,

> And not as Moses, which put a veil over his face, that the children of Israel could not steadfastly look to the end of that which is abolished: But their minds were blinded: for until this day remaineth the same veil untaken away in the reading of the old testament; which veil is done away in Christ. But even unto this day, when Moses is read, the veil is upon their heart. Nevertheless, when it shall turn to the Lord, the veil shall be taken away. Now the Lord is that Spirit; and where the Spirit of the Lord is, there is liberty.

To understand the meaning of the veil that Moses put over his face, we need to return to Exodus 34:34–35:

> But when Moses went in before the Lord to speak with him, he took the veil off, until he came out. And he came out, and spake unto the children of Israel that which he was commanded. And the children of Israel saw the face of Moses, that the skin of Moses' face shone: and Moses put the veil upon his face again, until he went in to speak to him.

The face of Moses radiated with the glory of the Lord, which man could not look on, requiring Moses to place a veil over his face. Moses himself did not directly see the face of God but was just exposed to God's glory as He passed by Moses. We read this in Exodus 33:22–23:

> And it shall come to pass, while my glory passeth by, that I will put thee in a clift of the rock, and will cover thee with my hand while I pass by: and I will take away mine hand, and thou shalt see my back parts: but my face shall not be seen.

These verses relate to the relationship God had with Moses as he led the people of Israel according to God's initial calling at the burning bush. Exodus 3:2–8 relates the account of how God appeared to Moses in a burning bush that was not consumed and stated, "I am the God of thy father, the God of Abraham, the God of Isaac, and the God of Jacob." God proceeded to tell Moses of His knowledge of the pain and sorrows of the children of Israel and how His people would be delivered from this bondage through Moses and taken out of Egypt to a land "flowing with milk and honey."

The children of Israel still have the veil over their eyes, as does anyone who does not know the Lord Jesus Christ as Savior. But we as believers are *in Christ*, as we examined in chapter 6. The contrast is between those *in Christ* who are under grace (2 Cor. 1:21–22: "Now he which stablisheth us with you in Christ, and hath anointed us is God; Who hath sealed us, and given the earnest of the Spirit in our hearts") and the nation of Israel who are under the law (2 Cor. 3:7: "But if the ministration of death, written and engraven in stones, was glorious, so that the children of Israel could not steadfastly behold the face of Moses for the glory of his countenance; which glory was to be done away").

All

The word "all," *pas* in the Greek, means "all, any, every, the whole." Simply stated, this word includes everyone who has placed their trust in the death, burial, and resurrection of Jesus Christ, not just a few chosen believers.

With Open Face

The word "open" is *anakalupto* in the Greek, which means "unveil." This word connects the preceding verses regarding the veil worn over Moses's face. This phrase relates to our position in Christ causing the veil to be lifted by the finished work of Christ on the cross and personally when our spiritual eyes are opened at our new birth.

Beholding in a Glass

The glass referred to here is the Word of God, which we are "rightly dividing" as we study and behold the truth. The beholding is not merely a mental assent of the truth, but an actual understanding, as our relationship with God through His glory is developed by our walk with the Lord Jesus Christ.

The Glory of the Lord

When we study the Word of God, we are actually beholding or becoming more aware of the character and ways of God, as manifested through the life and finished work on the cross by Jesus Christ and by His body of believers. The glory of God is recorded throughout the Scriptures as works, ways, encounters, metaphors, names, attributes, descriptive phrases, and "I am" statements. We should be vigilant as we study God's Word, capturing these aspects of God's glory.

Follow along in your Bible as we look at Colossians for an example of God's glory expressed as *works* (doctrines), beginning in Colossians 1:

- 1:2—sanctification
- 1:12—permanently qualified to partake of our inheritance
- 1:13—permanently delivered from dominion
- 1:13—permanently transformed to the Kingdom of the Son
- 1:14—redemption/forgiveness of sins
- 1:21—reconciliation
- 1:17—indwelling
- 2:12—identification in His death
- 2:12–13—raised with Him
- 2:14—all charges against us are nailed to the cross
- 2:15—spoiled principalities and powers
- 3:1–4—intercession at the right hand of God
- 3:1–4—permanently had hid our life with Him in God
- 3:10–11—removed racial, religious, cultural, social distinctions between believers.

God has given all these works, or doctrines, to us through the accomplishment of Jesus Christ on the cross.

Next, we explore two examples of the *ways* that God's glory is revealed to us in Scripture. The first example is 2 Corinthians 3:18, the current verse we are studying. As we proceed through the verse, we will see the extent of God's glory. The other example is Romans 12:2: "And be not conformed to this world: but be ye transformed by the renewing of your mind, that ye may prove what is that good, and acceptable, and perfect will of God." The actual transformation of the believer's mind demonstrates the glory of God through walking in the will of God and the workmanship that has been ordained in our lives. See Ephesians 2:10.

Encounters with God are often described as a meeting with the Angel of the Lord. Moses had a direct encounter with God, and that has been expatiated on in the first grouping of words under the heading "But We." Other encounters include Genesis 32:22–32 when Jacob wrestles with God, supported in verse 28: "Then the man said, 'Your name will no longer be Jacob, but Israel, because you have struggled with God and with humans and have overcome'" In the New Testament, people who recognized Jesus as the Messiah had an encounter with God. This list would include, but is not limited to, Mary the mother of Jesus, Joseph the husband of Mary, John the Baptist, the twelve apostles, and the thief on the cross. Following the resurrection, the apostle Paul saw the risen Lord on the road to Damascus.

When we search for *metaphors* that illustrate God's glory, a good place to begin your investigation is the book of Psalms. Looking at Psalm 18:1–2, we can locate several metaphors:

- my strength
- my rock
- my fortress
- my deliverer
- my shield
- the horn of my salvation
- my high tower

We know that God is not literally a rock, a fortress, or a shield. These words are used to enable us to see the glory of God manifested in earthly examples.

One of the most comprehensive studies regarding the glory of God is the *names* of the Lord. You will emerge from this study with a deeper relationship with your Lord as you study His names, of which there are many. In the book of Genesis 22:14, we have Jehovah-Jireh. This is interpreted as "The Lord will see to it. The Lord will provide." God's provision in this instance is a ram for a sacrifice in lieu of Isaac.

In Exodus 17:8–15, we meet Jehovah-Nissi: "the Lord is my banner." Moses gave that name to an altar that he erected upon a hill where he sat with uplifted hands during the successful battle against the Amalekites.

Next, we go to Judges 6:24 and discover Jehovah-Shalom: "the Lord is peace." This name was given to an altar erected by Gideon in Ophrah after God had given him the commission to deliver Israel from the Midianites.

Ezekiel 48:35 refers to Jehovah-Shammah, "the Lord is there." This name of the Lord relates to millennial Jerusalem as seen by Ezekiel in a vision.

In Psalm 113:1–3, we read one of many proclamations of the fruit of praise as manifested on the believer's lips: "Praise ye the Lord, Praise O ye servants of the Lord, praise the name of the Lord, Blessed be the name of the Lord from this time forth and for evermore. From the rising of the sun unto the going down of the same the Lord's name is to be praised."

Turning to the New Testament we look for the names of the Lord in a different sense. Beginning in John 1:1, we read, "In the beginning was the Word, and the Word was with God, and the Word was God." We clearly see that the progression of the Word equals God. Also in John 1:14, we see that "the Word was made flesh and dwelt among us, (and we beheld his glory, the glory as of the only begotten of the Father,) full of grace and truth." So, we can easily extrapolate that the Word who is God is Jesus Christ who came to earth as God the Son.

One of the most awesome portrayals of the names of God appears in Philippians 2: 9–11, which states, "Wherefore God also hath highly exalted him, and given him a name which is above every name: That at the name of Jesus every knee should bow, of things in heaven, and things in earth, and things under the earth; And that every tongue should confess that Jesus Christ is Lord, to the glory of God the Father." Here we see that God the Son is elevated above everything anywhere and someday everyone will confess Him as Lord on a bowed knee, some willingly and some in opposition.

Descriptions of God's *attributes* are exhaustive in the Bible. In Psalm 145 alone, we see many:

verse 3: inexhaustible and greatness
verse 7: goodness and righteousness
verse 8: gracious, full of compassion, long-suffering, and merciful
verse 13: everlasting dominion
verse 17: holy
verse 20: destroyer of the wicked

As you read God's Word, keep an account of all the attributes you find. Then take some time to meditate on each one. You will find this study to be richly rewarding in the renewal of your mind.

The next area to behold the glory of God is *descriptive phrases*. These are verses that expound on the wonderful manifestations of God. For instance, in Psalm 48:14 we read, "For this God is our God for ever and ever: he will be our guide even unto death." This phrase tells us something about our relationship with God. In Psalm 50:6 we read, "And the heavens shall declare his righteousness: for God is judge himself." One more in Psalm 54:4 states, "Behold, God is mine helper: the Lord is with them that uphold my soul." All of these powerful Scriptures should entice you to delve into the Word of God to extract more of these wondrous descriptions of God. There is a verse for anything you may be experiencing to provide comfort, peace, and freedom from fear and worry.

The last aspect of God's glory we will look at is the *"I am" statements*, found both in the Old and New Testaments. In Genesis 17:1 we read, "And when Abram was ninety years old and nine, the Lord appeared to Abram, and said unto him, I am the Almighty God; walk before me and be thou perfect." He is the self-existent One and has always been, neither created or formed.

In the book of Exodus, when God appears to Moses at a burning bush and instructs him to go to Pharaoh and lead the children out of Egypt, Moses asks

God who should he say sent him. God answers, "I AM THAT I AM: and he said, Thus shalt thou say unto the children of Israel, I AM hath sent me unto you." Again, God is stating that He has always existed.

In John 8:56 Jesus is addressing the Jews and states, "Your father Abraham rejoiced to see my day: and he saw it, and was glad." Verse 57 goes on to say, "Then said the Jews unto him, Thou art not yet fifty years old, and hast thou seen Abraham?" These Jews definitely understood what Jesus was saying. In verse 58 Jesus responds with a truth that causes the Jews to want to stone him for declaring He is God and existed before Abraham: "Verily, verily, I say unto you, Before Abraham was, I am."

Some of the most famous and compelling verses demonstrating the glory of God are found in the book of John. They are "I am" statements as well as *metaphors*. John 6:35 states, "I am the bread of life." Jesus is not really physical bread, but spiritual bread providing not physical sustenance but eternal life.

Looking at John 8:12, we read, "Then spake Jesus again unto them, saying, I am the light of the world: he that followeth me shall not walk in darkness, but shall have the light of life." Again, we know that Jesus was not really a physical light, but the spiritual light to lead us to all truth.

Another verse to see the combination of "I am" and metaphors is John 10:7, which states, "Then Jesus said unto them again, Verily, verily, I say unto you, I am the door of the sheep." As first glance the meaning would appear to be that Jesus is taking care of literal sheep, a concept that was clearly understood at the writing of the book of John. He is not an actual visible door. The spiritual meaning is of course that Jesus Christ is the only door or way to heaven.

There are several more of these combination verses that are worth extracting from the book of John. I encourage you to ferret them out and meditate on the meaning of those verses in your life.

Are Changed

The "rightly dividing" of these two seemingly uncomplicated words provides the ability to differentiate between a believer who remains in bondage to the concept of growing through works and the liberated follower of the Lord who understands the transformation by the Holy Spirit in the renewal of his mind.

The words "are changed" translate in the Greek to *metamorphoo* and mean "denoting a change of condition." Here in 2 Corinthians 3:18, the idea of transformation refers to an invisible or miraculous process in Christians that takes place or begins to take place in their life. The verb tense is present indicative middle, asserting something that is occurring while the speaker is making the statement. The middle voice represents the subject acting in some way upon himself or concerning himself.

What causes the change? According to the verb tense, the action is continuous, and the transformation is not visible to the human eye. God, of course, is quite aware of the change as it is occurring. We are transformed by feeding on the glory of God discovered in His Word, as we just explored in the last two sections of 2 Corinthians 3:18.

Into the Same Image

In chapter 4, under the heading "Progressive Sanctification," we examined Romans 8:29: "For whom he did foreknow, he also did predestinate to be conformed to the image of his Son, that he might be the first-born among many brethren." As believers, we are continuously being changed into the image of God's Son, as we manifest the fruit of the spirit of our prototype, the Lord Jesus Christ. Our *election* is as children of God, and our *predestination* is being conformed to the image of Jesus Christ as He is portrayed in the gospels of Matthew, Mark, Luke, and John. Jesus was the only person living on earth who was without sin after the fall of Adam and Eve in the Garden of Eden. As Romans 5:12 states, "Wherefore, as by one man sin entered into the world, and death by sin; and so death passed upon all men, for that all have sinned." The one man, of course, is Adam. It is stated in 2 Corinthians 5:21, "For he hath made him [Jesus] to be sin for us, who knew no sin; that we might be made the righteousness of God in him." And combining the truth of these two scriptures, we have a summary in Romans 5:17, which states, "For if by one man's offense death reigned by one; much more they which receive abundance of grace and of the gift of righteousness shall reign in life by one, Jesus Christ." As we grow in grace and righteousness, we are becoming more and more like Jesus Christ.

From Glory

Returning to the root/fruit principle, the Christian is rooted in the truth of Christ through "rightly dividing" God's Word. Studying the Word is a desire that the Lord infuses in our spiritual being and is executed over time.

To Glory

From the beholding of God's truth through "rightly dividing," the believer progresses through the four stages of growth and matures during his lifetime until the ultimate sanctification or glorification is reached. The fruit is manifested uniquely in each person as the Holy Spirit transforms the inner man through beholding the word of God.

Even As

These words actually mean "exactly as" and explain how we are changed from glory to glory.

By the Spirit of the Lord

Many Christians may begin and often continue their relationship with the Lord believing that in order to grow and become more Christlike, great effort to please God is essential. The way this belief is manifested may include reading the Bible at exactly the same time each morning for a certain period of study, or seeking God's favor by volunteering for several ministries in the church. What's really important, they think, is to obey God and work hard to do anything and everything possible in the church or community. These examples are not in any way disparaging to a believer, but are used to identify how we grow in our ongoing progressive sanctification process. We actually grow by the work of the Holy Spirit, who comes to reside within the believer at new birth in a way that humans don't really understand, but accept.

What or who is the Holy Spirit? To answer this question, we need to return to Genesis 1:26: "And God said, Let us make man in our image, after our likeness." The words "us" and "our" signify plurality of persons, which is depicted in the Godhead throughout scripture. Here we see the definite essence of God as the Father, Son, and Holy Spirit. God in the Hebrew is translated to *Elohim*, which has a plural connotation from the root *El*, or God. For the purposes of this book, however, the Holy Spirit will not be studied exhaustively, but will be explored as related to the believer's progressive sanctification. An extensive study of the Holy Spirit might be well worth pursuing in your Bible study or a Sunday school class in order to behold God's glory in this third person of the Godhead.

Throughout the Old Testament, the Holy Spirit is given and taken away from the follower of God for His glory. For example, in 1 Samuel 10:6, when the prophet Samuel is anointing Saul for the position of the first king of Israel, he states, "And the Spirit of the Lord will come upon thee, and thou shalt prophesy with them and shalt be turned into another man." We see this fulfilled in 1 Samuel 10:10: "And when they came thither to the hill, behold, a company of prophets met him [Saul]; and the Spirit of God came upon him and he prophesied among them." Samuel prophesied that Saul would receive the Holy Spirit, which would be evidenced by his ability to prophesy, and then we read the fulfillment when the Holy Spirit was actually given to Saul. Samuel, as a voice of the Lord, went to Saul and told him to attack Amalek and completely destroy all animals and people. Saul allowed Agag of the Amalekites to be spared. Samuel returned to Saul and confronted him with the disobedient act, saying, "Behold, to obey is better than sacrifice." Saul confessed his sin, but Samuel stated that Saul had rejected the Word of the Lord. The Lord was now rejecting Saul as the king of Israel and had already planned to bestow the kingship upon David. And in 1 Samuel 16:13 we read, "Then Samuel took the horn of oil, and anointed him in the midst of his brethren: and the Spirit of the Lord came upon David from that day forward." In the very next verse, we see the power of God: "But the Spirit of the Lord departed from Saul, and an evil spirit from the Lord troubled him."

After David committed his sin of adultery with Bath-Sheba, he penned the heart-baring Psalm 51 of confession and repentance. Verse 11 states, "Cast me not away from thy presence; and take not thy Holy Spirit from me." David knew that God could reject him as he rejected Saul, depending upon David's performance and behavior.

Today in the Body of Christ, we are secure because when we have accepted the Lord Jesus Christ as our Savior, we are "sealed with that holy Spirit of promise, which is the earnest of our inheritance until the redemption of the purchased possession, unto the praise of his glory" (Eph. 1:13–14). God will never take the Holy Spirit from us, because our salvation is not dependent upon our works but upon the finished work of our Savior, the Lord Jesus Christ. Titus 3:5 distinctly states, "Not by works of righteousness which we have done, but according to his mercy he saved us, by the washing of regeneration and renewing of the Holy Ghost."

The Holy Spirit's main functions in the life of a believer in the Body of Christ are to unveil the eyes of the Christian at the new birth, to lead us to behold the glory of the Lord in our lives, and to be the instrument of transformation as we continuously grow through the four progressive stages of our journey on the road to heaven.

The Apostle Paul

As believers, we will walk through many trials and circumstances on the way of our earthly pilgrimage. In order to understand this perspective, we turn to our most mature example in the Body of Christ, the apostle Paul. We have already examined the conversion of Saul the persecutor to Paul the apostle in relationship to the mystery of the Body of Christ in chapter 6.

Have you ever thought, "Paul is so perfect; I could never be like that"? When we compare ourselves to the Lord Jesus Christ, we all fall short. Paul had to grow in Christ, just as we do. So, let's look briefly at the progressive sanctification process of the apostle Paul.

Once Saul passed from death to life by the completed work of Jesus Christ on the cross, he was given a ministry as encapsulated in Acts 9:15: "He is a chosen vessel unto me, to bear my name before the Gentiles, and kings, and the children of Israel." We saw Saul become Paul as he was teaching in the synagogues and before kings, until he began his ultimate ministry as the apostle to the Gentiles. The pivotal verses as he transitions from preaching the Kingdom to teaching the Body of Christ are Acts 20:24–25: "But none of these things move me, neither count I my life dear unto myself, so that I might finish my course with joy, and the ministry, which I have received of the Lord Jesus, to testify the gospel of the grace of God. And now, behold, I know that ye all, among whom I have gone preaching the Kingdom of God, shall see my face no more."

By the words of his mouth, we can see that Paul has reached a level of maturity in the understanding of his purpose for serving the Lord at this point. Although we are unable to be precise, we can speculate that Paul understands the sovereignty of God's control in his life as he talks about "finishing his course with joy." At this point on the chronological timeline in the book of Acts, an accepted date is AD 57, which is the approximate time of the writing of the book of 2 Corinthians. Refer to chart 6 in the appendix, "Chronological Order of New Testament Books," to see where these books fit into the order of Paul's epistles from the New Testament. Paul often inserts himself into the Scriptures to support his teaching with the purpose of bringing glory to the Lord through His working in Paul's life.

Paul addresses his suffering as delineated in 2 Corinthians 11:24–28:

Of the Jews five times received I forty stripes save one. Thrice was I beaten with rods, once I was stoned, thrice I suffered shipwreck, a night and a day I have been in the deep; In journeyings often, in perils of waters, in perils of robbers, in perils by mine own countrymen, in perils by the heathen, in perils in the city, in perils in the wilderness, in perils in the sea, in perils among false brethren; In weariness and painfulness, in watchings, often, in hunger and thirst, in fastings often, in cold and nakedness. Beside those things that are without, that which cometh upon me daily, the care of all the churches.

Paul does not list these hardships to garner sympathy and portray a victim of dire circumstances, but to declare his suffering as a minister of Jesus Christ. He addresses the outward circumstances of persecutions and the daily administrations in the church as being equally valid to consider. Paul was not boasting in his ability to withstand these trials, and we can see that more clearly as he expounds in 2 Corinthians 12:1–10. Due to the importance of these verses related to our spiritual growth, they will be examined further for the relevance to our focus at this point:

> 1. It is not expedient for me doubtless to glory. I will come to visions and revelations of the Lord. 2. I knew a man in Christ above fourteen years ago, (whether in the body, I cannot tell; or whether out of the body, I cannot tell: God knoweth;) such a one caught up to the third heaven. 3. And I knew such a man, (whether in the body, or out of the body, I cannot tell: God knoweth;) 4. How that he was caught up into paradise, and heard unspeakable words, which it is not lawful for a man to utter. 5. Of such a one will I glory: yet of myself I will not glory, but in mine infirmities. 6. For though I would desire to glory, I shall not be a fool; for I will say the truth: but now I forbear, lest any man, should think of me above that which he seeth me to be, or that he heareth of me. 7. And lest I should be exalted above measure through the abundance of the revelations, there was given to me a thorn in the flesh, the messenger of Satan to buffet me, lest I should be exalted above measure. 8. For this thing I besought the Lord thrice, that it might depart from me. 9. And he said unto me, My grace is sufficient for thee: for my strength is made perfect in weakness. Most gladly therefore will I rather glory in my infirmities that the power of Christ may rest upon me. 10. Therefore I take pleasure in infirmities, in reproaches, in necessities, in persecutions, in distresses for Christ's sake: for when I am weak, then I am strong.

These ten verses are crucial to the understanding of God's love and protection as we walk through trials. In verses 1–4, we see the story of the apostle

Paul as fourteen years previously he was taken up to heaven where he saw things that were unspeakable. He referred to this as visions and revelations. The time that this occurred would have been approximately AD 43, probably shortly after Paul's conversion on the road to Damascus, very early in the progressive sanctification of Paul. The rapidity of a believer's growth is totally dependent upon the Lord's timetable for each individual. Paul was not sure if this was an out-of-body experience, but he seemed to accept that God knew.

When Paul states beginning in verse 5 that he would boast in this person, but not himself, I believe he is referring to the less mature Paul and contrasting his earlier level of beholding God's truth to the current time at the writing of 2 Corinthians in AD 57 when Paul understands his Lord better. Paul is saying that he doesn't want anyone to focus on him and exalt his exposure to the wonders of heaven. So, he continues to explain in verse 7 that because of the experience and caution of him being exalted for going to heaven, he received a thorn in the flesh to keep him humble. Much speculation has occurred regarding the identity of the thorn. Rather than discuss additional conjecture, I think the important takeaway here is that there was some debilitating malady thrust upon the apostle Paul to keep his focus on the Lord and his workmanship as a chosen vessel. Luke, the doctor, traveled with Paul, leading us to believe that the thorn might have been physical. If the specific condition was named, then we might say, "Oh, I don't have that," and miss the point of the entire narrative.

Paul prayed three times for the thorn to be removed in verse 8, which indicates that he was learning about the sovereignty of God at this point. The Lord's response to these prayers in verse 9 was not removal of the thorn to make Paul's life easier, but to provide sufficient grace for strength in Paul's weakness to enable him to walk through this trial.

I believe that Paul's response in verse 9 is his spiritual state at the time of the writing of this book in AD 57, although that is my opinion. This response demonstrates maturity regarding a difficult trial. So, Paul says he would rather boast in his weakness that the power of Christ may rest upon him, which would probably align his maturity growth level as a "young man" at this time.

He is other-focused and understands the sovereignty of God. He is grounded in the truth as he has been taught by the Lord Jesus Christ.

He expounds in verse 10 this beholding of freedom in Christ by boasting in the Lord and preferring the infirmities, reproaches, necessities, persecutions, and distresses to bring glory to the strength and power of God above the weakness of men.

Looking at verse 10 more closely, we see that "infirmities," or *astheneia* in the Greek, means "without strength." This is usually used in a comprehensive sense of the whole person, but it may also refer to a special form of bodily weakness or sickness.

The word "reproaches" is *hubris* in the Greek and means "insult, injury, harm, hurt, reproach." We use this word "hubris" in English to define pride or self-confidence.

Next the word "necessities" is *anagke* in the Greek and means "to bind hard or compress, constrict." It refers to necessity or compelling force, as opposed to willingness. These are the circumstances that appear to press in from all sides.

The word "persecutions" is *diogmos* and is translated "persecution." Paul speaks of persecution in the book of 2 Timothy, which was written about nine years after 2 Corinthians. At this point in his life, he had grown to the spiritual level of a "father" and was about to die. As you read 2 Timothy 3:10–12, compare this to 2 Corinthians 12:1–10. In 2 Timothy 3:10–12, Paul states, "10. But thou hast fully known my doctrine, manner of life, purpose, faith, long-suffering, charity, patience, 11. Persecutions, affliction, which came unto me at Antioch, at Iconium, at Lystra; what persecutions I endured: but out of them all the Lord delivered me. 12. Yea, and all that will live godly in Christ Jesus shall suffer persecution."

When you compare and contrast and 2 Corinthians 12:1–10 and 2 Timothy 3:10–12, you will see the progressive sanctification process that has taken place in Paul's life.

Paul states in 2 Corinthians that he desires to glorify God through the trials by demonstrating the strength and power of God through his weakness. Paul is attempting to teach us that trials will come to each Christian. We actually see a progression of suffering in verses 8–10, culminating in the five areas of trials that will make us more dependent upon the Lord. Trials actually demonstrate where we have been, where we are now, and where we are headed, based upon our reaction to them.

In 2 Timothy, Paul is listing a variety of the fruit to be found in the mature believer and saying that God is faithful to deliver a follower of Christ out of these persecutions that every believer "shall endure." Being delivered out of persecution does not always indicate the persecution will cease or decrease. The deliverance may be through additional grace to walk in the crucible or even death in this life, which is advancement to heaven. Paul succinctly addresses this truth in Philippians 1:21: "For me to live is Christ, and to die is gain."

Back to Alice Buffington and Heather Cook

Now that we have reviewed the transformation and renewed minds of the believer, using as a biblical example the apostle Paul, we need to examine our two Christian women who were introduced to us in chapter 2. To refresh your memory of Alice Buffington and Heather Cook, go back and read their descriptions and examples of a day in their lives from chapter 2.

Using the truths extracted from Romans 12:2, 2 Corinthians 3:18, and other scriptures perused, we might be able to extrapolate where Alice and Heather are headed in their individual walks with the Lord according to God's customized road map. Since Alice and Heather are contrived in the author's imagination, the projected continuation of each of their lives is subject to editing at any time.

Alice is presented as the more mature believer in her progressive sanctification process by the work of renewal and transformation of the Holy Spirit, which is supported by her study of God's Word, her focus on the Lord and His ministry for her life, and her concern with others and their need for a deeper relationship with the Lord. Alice has learned through various trials that dependency on the Lord rather than self is actually freedom and liberty from the bondage of sin and death. Based upon what we read of Alice's characteristics and observable fruit, she would probably be walking in the "father" stage. With that said, we must be circumspect to avoid a conclusion that Alice is so mature that she is never tempted to sin.

The apostle Paul very clearly admonishes us in the book of Philippians to never be deceived in believing that we have arrived at a level of perfection. Beginning in chapter 3 verse 12, we read, "Not that I had already attained, either were already perfect: but I follow after, if that I may apprehend that for which I am apprehended of Christ Jesus." Continuing in verse 13 into 14, Paul illuminates, "Brethren, I count not myself to have apprehended: but this one thing I do, forgetting those things which are behind, and reaching forth unto those things which are before, I press toward the mark for the prize of the high calling of God in Christ Jesus."

Chart 10 in the appendix, "Sin and Growth," helps clarify what Paul is describing in Philippians. When we are "transformed from death to life" by the completed work of Jesus Christ on the cross, our "old man or body of sin has been destroyed" (Rom. 6:6), and we are "walking in newness of life" (Rom. 6:4). As Paul has stated, however, we have not attained perfection and still are capable of sinning. The diagram depicts our projected sin from the cross to heaven as we are continuously being conformed to the image of Jesus Christ (Rom. 8:29). The sin, represented by the lines and peaks, decreases proportionately to the renewal of our minds as represented by the downward trend and shorter lines and peaks. But we have occurrences of sinful behavior (peaks) and temporary plateaus (straight lines). If we could graph the lives of several Christians, each chart would be the same as far as the decrease of sin, but the peaks would differ according to the trials experienced. Also, the individual plan of each believer varies according to the workmanship ordained by God (Eph. 2:10).

From the description of Heather, she is obviously the less mature believer. Heather has a love for God and His Word, but she is often stressed by her circumstances and the belief that Satan has more influence over her life than he really does. She tends to listen to the fiery darts of accusation being hurled at her and forgets about the shield of faith. At this point in her life, she does not see that God is completely in control of every aspect of her life. Also, Heather is more concerned about what God is doing in her life than placing the needs of others first. She appears to be a good mother and wants the best for her children, but she has not been refined to the point of solid maturity. According to the characteristics and observable fruit in Heather's life, we would place her in the "young child" stage of progressive sanctification as the Holy Spirit is leading her through various trials and purging out the dross of sin.

This is a good point at which to review the reality of examining the level of growth. Alice and Heather are presented in pure stages, but often believers are overlapping in the growth stages. Avoid looking at those believers around you and assigning them to a particular level of growth. The purpose of learning about the growth stages is to understand progressive sanctification in your own life and to receive encouragement for being exactly where God has you at your stage in the Christian life. Knowing this liberating truth will help you avoid the condemnation that often occurs when one believer begins to judge the life of another Christian. Paul very succinctly assuages any unfavorable labeling of another believer in Romans 8:1: "There is therefore now no condemnation to them which are in Christ Jesus, who walk not after the flesh, but after the Spirit." The operative words are "who walk not after the flesh," which distinguish the unbeliever from the believer who walks "after the Spirit."

Our walk with the Lord may vacillate between peaks of great joy and valleys of discouragement or sorrow, but we are always moving forward and closer to the image of our Lord and Savior Jesus Christ. Knowing the truth of our location on the road to heaven will provide a rewarding Christian life of liberty and freedom to serve the Lord as He has always intended us to do.

Questions for Group Discussion or Individual Study

1. What do you believe is the function of the pastor of a church? Does your pastor fulfill these functions? If not, what would you like to have him change? Do you encourage your pastor and his family? Often, we can see the need for change in others, but we do not see how God may use us in a situation.

2. Explain the root/fruit principle that Paul uses in his epistles. Give some scriptural examples. When do you believe spiritual growth begins in a Christian?

3. 2 Corinthians 3:18 was examined to clarify our transformation and renewal processes. Explain in your own words the meaning of this verse and how studying this verse has changed your understanding of Christian growth.

4. Within 2 Corinthians 3:18 are several ministudies. One of these is to explore the glory of the Lord related to works, ways, encounters, metaphors, names, attributes, descriptive phrases, and "I am" statements. If you have not already begun using a notebook to record these characteristics of God's glory, begin to do this today. You will reap extensive spiritual blessings.

5. Another ministudy would be to look at the myriad of Scriptures describing the Holy Spirit. Compare and contrast what you find to assist your understanding of the unique working of this third person of the Godhead. Can the Holy Spirit be taken away from a believer? Why or why not? Use Scriptures to defend your answer.

6. We examined the progressive sanctification of the apostle Paul. Do you think that Paul is any different from any other believer? Should we exalt Paul in any way? Whom should we exalt? Why? A deeper study about Paul would be to form a timeline of his life and to use chart 6 and the book of Acts.

7. When Paul was describing his trials and the thorn in the flesh, did you identify your own progressive sanctification process and see how God's grace has been sufficient in your life? Have you ever suffered

persecution? Sometimes we equate persecution with physical hardships and martyrdom. There are many types of persecution. Stop and make a list of what you have learned in your walk with the Lord up to now. If you are studying this book in a group, this would be a good time to share your testimonies with the others for encouragement.

8. When you reviewed the characteristics and lives of Alice Buffington and Heather Cook, did you see anything differently than when you initially read chapter 2. If so, what did you see?

9. Are you able to relate the four growth stages of progressive sanctification to the lives of Alice and Heather? How about your life? Sometimes we tend to place ourselves further along in our growth than we really are.

10. Think about chart 10. Had you ever studied or been taught about the decrease of sin in a believer's life as she grows and is becoming more like Jesus Christ? Do you think you could ever achieve a life of sinless perfection on this earth? Defend your answer with Scripture. Do you have a better understanding of where you fit into God's plan for your life after reading the first seven chapters of this book? I encourage you to continue to study with the purpose of "rightly dividing" the Word of God. You will be transformed, renewed, and be a mature "tree," bearing beautiful fruit for your Lord and Savior Jesus Christ.

8

If You Don't Know the Lord, Then...

*For by grace are ye saved through faith; and that not of yourselves;
it is the gift of God: Not of works, lest any man should boast. For
we are his workmanship, created in Christ Jesus unto good works,
which God hath before ordained that we should walk in them.*

—EPHESIANS 2:8–10

After reading the preceding seven chapters of this book, some of you may not understand the essence of the truth "rightly divided" regarding spiritual discernment of the tenets of the Christian faith. Many questions about the need to know this information garnered from the Word of God may be foremost in your mind:

- "What does all this have to do with me? What I have read does not make any sense related to my life and how I live."
- "Why should I consider anything in the Bible, because it was written so long ago and doesn't even apply to the world as I see it? I am doing well in my life."
- "Why should I need a crutch like religion? I am strong and depend on my intelligent thinking in life's situations."

Since answers to biblical questions are found in the Bible, turn with me to 1 Corinthians, where the apostle Paul addresses these same concerns. In chapter 1 Paul is talking about preaching the gospel to the two groups of people acknowledged in his time: the Jews and everyone else, referred to as Gentiles or Greeks. Read these verses a few times and think about what they are saying to you.

1 Corinthians 1:17–27:

17. For Christ sent me not to baptize, but to preach the gospel: not with wisdom of words, lest the cross of Christ should be made of none effect. 18. For the preaching of the cross is to them that perish foolishness: but unto us which are saved it is the power of God. 19. For

it is written, I WILL DESTROY THE WISDOM OF THE WISE, AND WILL BRING TO NOTHING THE UNDERSTANDING OF THE PRUDENT. 20. Where is the wise? Where is the scribe? Where is the disputer of this world? Hath not God made foolish the wisdom of this world? 21. For after that in the wisdom of God the world by wisdom knew not God, it pleased God by the foolishness of preaching to save them that believe. 22. For the Jews require a sign, and the Greeks seek after wisdom; 23. But we preach Christ crucified, unto the Jews a stumbling block, and unto the Greeks foolishness. 24. But unto them which are called, both Jews and Greeks, Christ the power of God, and the wisdom of God. 25. Because the foolishness of God is wiser than men; and the weakness of God is stronger than men. 26. For ye see your calling, brethren, how that not many wise men after the flesh, not many mighty, not many noble, are called: 27. But God hath chosen the foolish things of the world to confound the wise; and God hath chosen the weak things of the world to confound the things which are mighty.

These powerful words resonate in the hearts of those individuals who have put their trust in the Lord Jesus Christ as Savior. What a contrast between the former life as an unbeliever with the inability to truly behold the truths of God's Word, and a "new creature" *in Christ* able to study the Bible and be transformed in the mind with resultant wisdom and knowledge for a life dependent upon the Lord Jesus Christ.

As we unpack 1 Corinthians 1:17–27, read with an open mind and listen to what God is divinely trying to impart to your mind and eventually to your heart. As we have explored in earlier chapters, the apostle Paul was a chosen vessel to preach the gospel to the nation of Israel, kings, and most importantly to the Gentiles. We see in verse 17 that he was not focusing on water baptism but on the baptism of the Holy Spirit given to the believer at the moment of salvation. Paul emphasizes that the gospel is not words of wisdom, but the focus is on the finished work of Jesus Christ as He died on the cross for our sins. To the unbeliever, the truth of the sacrifice of the cross is foolish, but to those of us who have been saved, the cross is the power of the resurrection in which we walk as believers. This power gives us great joy, peace, and liberty to serve the Lord.

Paul continues in verse 19 with a quote from Isaiah 29:14 regarding wisdom of the world versus that of God. Looking at verse 22, we see that the Jews require a sign and the Greeks are looking for wisdom. Paul further expounds in the remaining verses that the gospel is a stumbling block to the Jews and to the wise Greeks, foolishness. Foolishness in the world was chosen by God to cause shame to the wise and weakness to cause shame to the mighty. God's ways are often incompatible with the ways of the natural man. Christians may be considered weak, or intolerant, or narrow-minded by the world because of adherence to the inerrancy of Scripture rather than following the socially acceptable trends of the day.

In the book of Romans, the apostle Paul effectively contrasts the natural, or lost, to the spiritual, or saved, conditions of men. He begins Romans 7 with what I believe is his personal testimony. In verses 7–25, we read,

7. What shall we say then? Is the law sin? Nay, I had not known sin, but by the law: for I had not known lust, except the law had said, THOU SHALT NOT COVET. 8. But sin, taking occasion by the commandment, wrought in me all manner of concupiscence. For without the law sin was dead. 9. For I was alive without the law once: but when the commandment came, sin revived, and I died. 10. And the commandment, which was ordained to life, I found to be unto death. 11. For sin, taking occasion by the commandment, deceived me, and by it slew me. 12. Wherefore the law is holy, and the commandment holy, and just, and good. 13. Was then that which is good made death unto me? God forbid. But sin, that it might appear sin, working death in me by that which is good; that sin by the commandment might become exceedingly sinful. 14. For we know that the law is spiritual: but I am carnal sold under sin. 15. For that which I do I allow not; for what I would, that do I not; but what I hate, that do I. 16. If then I do that which I would not, I consent unto the law that it is good. 17.

Now then it is no more I that do it, but sin that dwelleth in me. 18. For I know that in me (that is in my flesh) dwelleth no good thing: for to will is present with me: but how to perform that which is good I find not. 19. For the good that I would I do not; the evil which I would not, that I do. 20. Now if I do that I would not, it is no more I that do it, but sin that dwelleth in me. 21. I find then a law, that, when I would do good, evil is present with me. 22. For I delight in the law of God after the inward man: 23. But I see another law in my members warring against the law of my mind, and bringing me into captivity to the law of sin which is in my members. 24. O wretched man that I am! Who shall deliver me from the body of this death. 25. I thank God through Jesus Christ our Lord. So then with the mind I myself serve the law of God; but with the flesh the law of sin.

Romans 7 has been the source of much confusion. If you read several commentaries, you will discover various interpretations of the meaning of verses 7–25. My intention is not to muddy the waters any further, but to clarify the difference between a lost and saved human being according to my personal "rightly dividing" of the scriptures and not based upon any other person's commentaries or opinion. I strongly recommend that you study these passages and the ones following in Romans 8 to "rightly divide" them for your own satisfaction.

Rather than parsing each verse, I will present an overall summary of groups of verses. In verses 7–12 Paul's main thrust is to explain that the law itself is not sin, but it exposes the sinful nature of man and defines the area of the sin committed. The law was holy and given to Moses by God in the form of the Ten Commandments. Read Exodus chapter 20 to review the law that was ordained for the nation of Israel to follow out of obedience to God. For example, Leviticus 26:3–4 states, "*If* ye walk in my statutes, and keep my commandments, and do them; *Then* I will give you rain in due season," as a conditional statement elaborating in subsequent verses on threshing and sowing abundance, peace in the land, safety from enemies, respect, setting the tabernacle among the people, and walking among the people and being their

God. If the nation of Israel walks in disobedience, Leviticus 26:14–15 states, "But if ye will not hearken unto me, and will not do all these commandments, And if ye shall despise my statutes, or if your soul abhor my judgments, so that ye will not do all my commandments, but that ye break my covenant," and the list follows with the consequences of disobedience through the end of chapter 26. When you read these remaining Scriptures, the apparent conditional ramifications of disobedience become very clear.

We have already examined the function of the law as a schoolmaster to bring us to Christ, which demonstrates that no one could keep the law. In James 2:10 this becomes clear: "For whosoever shall keep the whole law, and yet offend in one point, he is guilty of all." In the Old Testament, the desire to follow God and keep the commandments demonstrated the believer's true heart for obedience.

By returning to chapter 6 and reading the sections titled "The Gospel," "Salvation and the Body of Christ," and "Justification," you will have a good review of how the law as given to Moses is differentiated from the grace of God as given to the Body of Christ.

Romans 7:13–20 shows the progression of how Paul's sinful nature affected his outward behavior. In verse 14 he very clearly states that he is "carnal, *sold under sin.*" Carnality is a synonym for the lost state of all persons at the time of birth. If a person becomes a Christian through the new birth, then he is in a permanent state of being saved from his sin. This salvation is solely achieved through faith in the death, burial, and resurrection of the Lord Jesus Christ.

Beginning in verse 15, Paul talks about the inability to do the things that are good but doing what he really hates. The cause: sin that dwells within him. In the lost state, a person is in bondage to sin to serve the desires of the "old man," which is also referred to as the "sin nature."

In verses 18–20, Paul says there is no good thing dwelling in him and he is quite capable of doing only that which is evil due to the indwelling sin. This is a man with a God-given conscience who has a desire to do what is right but knows that he is helpless to do so.

Finally, in verses 21–22, we see man who realizes the law given by God is good, but the "sin nature" present in a lost man gives him a propensity toward evil and captivity to a life of sin. He acknowledges that he is wretched and sinful and cries out for deliverance from the "sinful nature" or "body of death." Then, he has his eyes opened to the truth that "Jesus Christ our Lord" is the answer to break free from the bondage of sin. Paul has actually already presented this truth in Romans 6:6: "Knowing this, that our old man is crucified with him, that the body of sin might be destroyed, that henceforth we should not serve sin." The Greek word *katargeo* for the word "destroyed" means to "render entirely idle, abolish, cease, do away, vanish away." The connotation of all of these meanings would indicate annihilation of the "sin nature." The verb tense for "be destroyed" is aorist subjunctive passive, which refers to simple, undefined action occurring at a specific point in time, as opposed to continuous or repeated action.

As we examine what the apostle Paul is saying, we see the drawing toward salvation of a lost man by the Holy Spirit as was expounded in chapter 3 under the headings "Prejustification Sanctification" and "Justifying Sanctification." We witness his veil "being lifted" as he sees the total depravity of his sin and then the answer to freedom from this bondage. The answer is the Lord Jesus Christ.

Romans 8:1 contains the word "therefore," which always signals the reader to examine the preceding verses for the context of meaning. We have just scrutinized the verses in Romans 7 to determine the transformation of Paul from darkness to light.

Now, we will contrast the lost and saved man in Romans 8:1–14:

1. There is therefore now no condemnation to them which are in Christ Jesus, who walk not after the flesh, but after the Spirit. 2. For the law of the Spirit of life in Christ Jesus hath made me free from the law of sin and death. 3. For what the law could not do, in that it was weak through the flesh, God sending his own Son in the likeness of sinful flesh, and for sin, condemned sin in the flesh. 4. That the righteousness of the law might be fulfilled in us, who walk not after the flesh, but after the Spirit. 5. For they that are after flesh do mind the things of the flesh; but they that are after the Spirit the things of the Spirit. 6. For to be carnally minded is death; but to spiritually minded is life and peace. 7. Because

the carnal mind is enmity against God: for it is not subject to the law of God, neither indeed can be. 8. So then they that are in the flesh cannot please God. 9. But ye are not in the flesh, but in the Spirit, if so be that the Spirit of God dwell in you, Now if any man have not the Spirit of Christ, he is none of his. 10. And if Christ be in you, the body is dead because of sin; but the Spirit is life because of righteousness. 11. But if the Spirit of him that raised up Jesus from the dead dwell in you, he that raised up Christ from the dead shall also quicken your mortal bodies by his Spirit that dwelleth in you. 12. Therefore, brethren, we are debtors, not to the flesh, to live after the flesh. 13. For if ye live after the flesh, ye shall die: but if ye through the Spirit do mortify the deeds of the body, ye shall live. 14. For as many as are led by the Spirit of God, they are the sons of God.

These fourteen verses are crucial to understanding the position we have in Christ when we have been redeemed out of the condition of bondage to sin. Look at chart 11 in the appendix, "Contrast of Lost and Saved," to assist you in parsing the verses.

We will examine each point to elaborate for clarification. The *first contrast* is from Romans 8:1, where we see that based upon Paul's testimony in chapter 7, there is no condemnation for the saved members of the Body of Christ, because their lifestyle is one that reflects the work of the Holy Spirit as fruit. This fruit is listed in Galatians 5:22–23 as "love, joy, peace, long-suffering, gentleness, goodness, faith." The lost are walking in a lifestyle as described in Galatians 5:19–20 as the works of the flesh, "adultery, fornication, uncleanness, lasciviousness, idolatry, witchcraft, hatred, variance, emulations, wrath, strife, seditions, heresies."

Remember that a Christian has not arrived in a state of perfection and continues with the capacity to sin, but his lifestyle will produce fruit and godly behavior, not a daily walk in the works of the flesh, because of the liberty a believer has in Christ through the work of the Holy Spirit.

The *second point* in chart 11 comes from Romans 8:2–3, which clearly states that when we become Christians, we are freed from the bondage of sin and death that controls the lost man. The nation of Israel could not keep the law due to the sin nature and inability to walk in righteousness apart from the indwelling Holy Spirit. Jesus Christ, who was God the Son, came to earth as a man without sin to condemn sin through death on the cross. Since the appearance of the Holy Spirit as described in Acts 2, the believer has been able to walk in "newness of life," rather than trying to follow the law as the apostle Paul preached first to the Jews and then to the Gentiles.

The righteousness of the law is actually fulfilled in the believer, who has the indwelling Holy Spirit and walks in power of the Spirit, in contrast to the unbeliever who walks continuously in the flesh, or sin nature. *Point three* in chart 11, from Romans 8:4, alludes to this truth. What liberty to be led in our daily walk with the Lord through the renewing of our minds by the Holy Spirit, rather than trying to keep the law by the works of the flesh, which is exhausting and frustrating, generating behavior that is not pleasing to the Lord!

When we examine *point four* in chart 11 related to Romans 8:5, the clarity of contrast is quite striking. The lost man who does not know the Lord will follow his own desires and sin quite easily, often without any regrets. Although he may believe that his life is pursuant with good intentions, Jesus tells us clearly in John 15:5, "I am the vine, ye are the branches: He that abideth in me, and I in Him, the same bringeth forth much fruit: for without me ye can do nothing." So, without the indwelling Holy Spirit that comes with new birth, a person is not able to do anything good. Paul also addresses this truth in Romans 3:12, where he quotes Psalm 14:3: "THEY ARE ALL GONE OUT OF THE WAY, THEY ARE TOGETHER BECOME UNPROFITABLE; THERE IS NONE THAT DOETH GOOD, NO, NOT ONE." An unbeliever is not capable of doing anything good as God defines good. In the eyes of the world, many individuals have performed service and acts of kindness that have garnered praise. According to God's Word, if they were not done by a Christian, they were not good. We can convince ourselves that we are kind and loving, but human love is totally different than God's love that is "shed abroad in our hearts by the Holy Spirit," as we read in Romans 5:5. When our spiritual eyes are opened by the Holy Spirit to see that we need the Lord, our lives are changed forever. When becoming believers, we need to remember that we were unbelievers at one time and that the only difference between the lost and the saved person is faith in the finished work of the Lord Jesus Christ on the cross. The apostle Paul is wise to exhort believers with this truth in Ephesians 2:2–3: "Wherein in time past ye walked according to the course of this world, according to the prince of the power of the air, the spirit, that now worketh in the children of disobedience. Among whom also we all had our conversation in times past in the lusts of our flesh, fulfilling the desires of the flesh and of the mind; and were by nature the children of wrath, even as others." The enemy of God and the believer is Satan, who is directing the paths of the unbeliever to fulfill his desires through circumstances and by the thoughts of the mind. We need to acknowledge that Satan exists but remember that he is a created being. God is sovereign over all creation, including Satan. We have discussed this truth in prior chapters and will not pursue it further at this time.

Progressing to *point five* in chart 11, which relates to Romans 8:6, we see that the end result for the lost person is eternal death and ultimate separation from God, while the saved person anticipates eternal life in heaven with God. The apostle John clearly pens this truth in John 3:36: "He that believeth on the Son hath everlasting life: and he that believeth not the Son shall not see life; but the wrath of God abideth on him." You might say, I understand that life means going to heaven, but what is the wrath of God? Let's go quickly to the book of Revelation, which expounds upon various judgments concerning seals, trumpets, plagues, and vials in chapters 6–16, with the final judgment in chapter 20, verses 10–15:

And the devil that deceived them was cast into the lake of fire and brimstone, where the beast and the false prophet are, and shall be tormented day and night forever and ever. And I saw a great white throne, and him that sat on it, from whose face the earth and the heaven fled away; and there was found no place for them. And I saw the dead, small and great, stand before God; and the books were opened: and another book was opened, which is the book of life: and the dead were judged out of those things which were written in the books, according to their works. And the sea gave up the dead which were in it; and death and hell delivered up the dead which were in them: and they were judged every man according to their works. And death and hell were cast into the lake of fire. This is the second death. And whosoever was not found written in the book of life was cast into the lake of fire.

Many people believe that when we die physically, we just stop existing and that is the end of life. As you have just read, that is very far from the reality of what is going to happen. If you have not received the Lord Jesus Christ as your Savior, through acceptance of his death, burial, and resurrection, you will appear before God and be judged according to your works on earth. As we have just seen from God's Word, that any work performed apart from the leading of the Holy Spirit is not good. This individual will not be found in the Lamb's book of life, which determines the final destination to be the lake of fire along with the devil and his angels. It won't be a party in hell with your buddies, but total separation from God. Try to imagine the isolation and agony that will be experienced for eternity.

As you have learned while reading in this book, a relationship with Jesus Christ begins with believing in the gospel. In its simplest form, we see the death of Jesus on the cross as the only acceptable payment for the sin of man, His burial as evidence of his death, and His resurrection ensuring the power to raise the believer from the death and bondage of sin. Since all believers are in the Lamb's book of life, any Christian will not experience the second death but will live for eternity in heaven.

The most important takeaway from this explanation of what happens when you die is to behold that you will live somewhere forever. Do you want to live in torment and separated from God, or do you want to live in total glorification with the Lord and other Christians in a place that God is preparing for those who belong to Him?

Looking at Romans 8:7, which corresponds to *point number six* in chart 11, we see the contrast of the lost being God's enemy and the saved being the redeemed of God. Think about what that is actually saying. If you don't know the Lord, you are an enemy of God. That is a very frightening concept, don't you think? But you say, "Isn't God a God of love?" The answer to that question is a resounding yes! Look at 1 John 4:7–10: "Beloved, let us love one another: for love is of God; and every one that loveth is born of God, and knoweth God. He that loveth not knoweth not God; for God is love. In this was manifested the love of God toward us, because that God sent his only begotten Son into the world, that we might live through him. Herein is love, not that we love God, but that he loved us, and sent his Son to be the propitiation for our sins." The word "propitiation" is *hilasmos* in the Greek, which means "atonement, or an expiator." This word indicates "not only the benefit of reconciliation, but the manner whereby sinners are made friends of God." *Hilasmos* refers to Christ as the one "who propitiates and offers himself as the propitiation." Only the sacrifice of Jesus Christ on the cross was acceptable to God for the atonement of our sin. The ultimate expression of God's love was the sacrifice of God the Son.

God is love and also is a righteous judge. Jesus is the mediator between God and man to provide a way toward an eternal relationship that can never be broken. We read in 1 Timothy 2:5, "For there is one God, and one mediator between God and men, the man Christ Jesus." The relationship with God, not a religion, is what generates peace and identity that will stand against any foe.

Point seven in chart 11 corresponds to Romans 8:8 and clearly makes the case for not being able to please God if you are unsaved. Those who have received the Lord Jesus are pleasing to God, because their life is one of service as led by the working of the Holy Spirit. We can be sure of our relationship with God because of what Jesus did, as found in Ephesians 2:15, "having abolished in his flesh the enmity"; only by walking in the light of Christ are we able to be pleasing to God.

To elaborate on *point eight* in chart 11 which corresponds to Romans 8:9, we see that the unsaved person does not have the indwelling Holy Spirit, while the saved believer does have the indwelling Holy Spirit. A clear indicator of having a relationship with God is the presence of the Holy Spirit. Ephesians 1:13 says, "In whom ye also trusted after that ye heard the word of truth, the gospel of your salvation in whom also after that ye believed, ye were sealed with that holy Spirit of promise." When an important dispatch was written by a king, he affixed a waxed seal to it to ensure that only the intended person would open the letter. If an inappropriate person opened the letter, the breaking of the seal would be evident. When God has sealed the believer with the Holy Spirit, nothing can break the seal. That is eternal security!

Looking at *point nine* in chart 11, verses 10–11 refer to the death of the body because of sin with no spiritual life in a nonbeliever and the curse of sin on the believer's physical body in this lifetime, but the life of the resurrected body by the Holy Spirit that dwells in the believer. It is chilling to contemplate the contrast between the state of bondage throughout life as a sinner (Rom. 3:23) with the life of freedom in Christ as a saint set apart when you belong to the Lord (2 Cor. 3:17).

Finally, *point 10* in chart 11 provides us with a clear picture of the separation of the lost man from God compared to the position of the saved man as a son of God. Verses 12–14 stipulate that a Christian is no longer indebted to sin to live as the lost who will surely die. But through the transformation of the Holy Spirit, growth will occur to live above the worldly lifestyle. This contrast is stated succinctly in Romans 6:23: "For the wages of sin is death; but the gift of God is eternal life through Jesus Christ our Lord." The death referred to in this verse of course, since everyone faces physical death, is the eternal separation from God and destination in the lake of fire as was discussed earlier.

Death or life? Which do you prefer? You may ask, "How can you prove this to me? Who has ever returned from the dead to corroborate these speculations?" My answer is simple. I cannot prove it, but I know that it is true. God's Word is replete with Scriptures addressing all of the different truths that have been discussed in this book. You need to study and "rightly divide" the Word. You may be quite astonished to behold these truths as God opens your eyes of understanding. Faith is what a Christian holds on to. Hebrews 11:1 defines faith in a most intangible way: "Now faith is the substance of things hoped for, the evidence of things not seen." Think about what you are reading. What is your faith in? What do you hope for? I have been praying for you as a reader as I wrote this book. God has put this book in your hands, and I hope you will be excited about reading the Bible and joining a Bible study. Whether you already know the Lord or are discovering His bountiful treasures for the first time, I pray that God will use what you have read for His glory in your life.

Now you have seen the Christian's journey on the road to heaven. God is taking you along the way at the pace He has designed for you individually. Thank you for taking this long walk with me as we discovered, reviewed, and reflected upon the wonderful and precious elucidation of our spiritual growth. Remember you are exactly where you are meant to be at this time in your life. I can't wait to meet those of you who will be in heaven with me someday!

Questions for Group Discussion or Individual Study

1. Explain in your own words what Paul is delineating in 1 Corinthians 1:17–27. Reread the Scriptures to refresh your memory. What does he mean when he says that the Jews require a sign? Or that the Greeks seek after wisdom?

2. Do you believe that anyone is able to pick up a Bible and truly understand the meaning of Scripture? Why or why not? Defend your answer from 1 Corinthians 1:17–27. You may use any other verses as well.

3. Return to Romans 7:7–25 and carefully read these verses. Who do you think is speaking here? About whom is he speaking? Can you relate to these verses in your life? What are you trusting in for your life? Do you have contentment in your life? Do you trust your choices and judgment in the circumstances that occur?

4. Is the death, burial, and resurrection of the Lord Jesus Christ foolishness to you? Can you explain why or why not? Have you ever thought about the validity of this truth? If you have, do you read the Bible to either disprove or affirm your conclusion?

5. Romans chapter 8 is an extensive study about the differences between the lost and the saved, transitioning into the glorious security believers have in their relationship with God. Review chart 11 beginning with points 1 and 2. Explain in your own words the contrast between walking in the flesh and in the spirit, and bondage versus freedom from sin. Be sure to study the corresponding verses in Romans 8:1–3.

6. Look at points 3 and 4 of chart 11 carefully, and relate unrighteousness with righteousness and focusing on fleshly things with a spiritual focus. Romans 8:4–5 will assist you in your study. You may want to find other Scriptures supporting these issues.

7. Points 5 and 6 of chart 11 dealing with death and life of the spirit and the contrast of being God's enemy or God's redeemed present very crucial support for the eternal destiny of all people and our actual

standing with God. Refer to Romans 8: 6-7 for clarification of these points.

8. Romans 8: 8-9 refer to the contrast between the flesh and the Spirit summarized in points 7 and 8 of chart 11. Read these verses very carefully and relate them to your position concerning God.

9. The remaining verses of Romans 8:10-14 contain some deep doctrinal truth regarding the work of Jesus Christ in a life and the transition from spiritual death to life. You might read the accounts of the crucifixion and resurrection in the books of Mathew (27–28), Mark (15–16), Luke (23–24), and John (19–20) at this time to enter into the depth of these verses in Romans. Remember that the accounts are not identical because they are written by four different eyewitnesses.

10. Now that you have read the entire book, and especially this final chapter, do you believe your name would be in the lost or saved column in chart 11? Explain how you derived your answer. God and you are the only ones who can answer that question truthfully. If you are unable to place your name in the saved column, continue to read the Bible and talk to people you know who belong to the Body of Christ.

Appendix

Chart 1

Summary of Verse Analysis on 2 Corinthians 3:18

BUT WE: contrast between those IN CHRIST (2 Corinthians 1:21-22) under grace and the Nation of Israel (2 Corinthians 3:7) under the law.

ALL: all believers, not a chosen few.

WITH OPEN FACE: veil is lifted by the finished work of Jesus Christ on the cross and personally when our spiritual eyes are opened at our new birth.

BEHOLDING IN A GLASS: A work by the Spirit of God as teacher to reveal truths of Jesus Christ to the believer as they "look into the Word of God" through study "to shew themselves approved". This idea goes beyond mental assent to actually understanding Glory through a continuously developing relationship with God through the Lord Jesus Christ.

THE GLORY OF THE LORD: The character and ways of God as exhibited (1) through the person and work of Christ to and through the believers and (2) recorded in Scripture as works; ways; encounters; metaphors; names; attributes; descriptive phrases; I-am statements.

ARE CHANGED

Metamorphosed

    (1) Miraculous/continuous action verb

    (2) Fruit of life

    (3) By feeding on glory through meditation

INTO THE SAME IMAGE: exhibiting the fruit of Jesus Christ our prototype

FROM GLORY	**TO GLORY**	**EVEN AS**	**BY THE SPIRIT OF**
Rooted in truth	Resulting in	exactly as	**THE LORD**
of Jesus Christ	a fruit in the		The work of God's
manifested to the	believer		Spirit
believer	Progressing to		(1) The unveiling of eyes
	glorification		in new birth
			(2) The perception of
			glory
			(3) The transformation

Printed with acknowledgment to Donna Stamey Carver for permission

Chart 2

Sanctification

(*hagiasmos*—separation unto God)

I. Prejustification sanctification (2 Thess. 2:13–14)
   A. Work of the Holy Spirit to protect the elect until salvation
   B. Bringing the elect under the hearing of the gospel
   C. Opening up the understanding of the elect
   D. Giving the gift of faith through the hearing of the Word
II. Justifying sanctification (Acts 26:18)
   A. The setting apart of the believer into the Body of Christ *at the time* they trust the Lord Jesus Christ as their Savior
III. Progressive sanctification (Rom. 8:29, John 17:17)
   A. The believer is set apart by God for a purpose.
   B. The believer is set apart by the Word of God.
IV. Ultimate sanctification (Phil. 3:21)
   A. The believer is set apart in heaven.

(Printed with acknowledgment to Donna Stamey Carver for permission.)

Chart 3

Old Man/New Man

THEREFORE IF ANY MAN BE IN CHRIST, HE IS A NEW CREATION: OLD

THINGS ARE PASSED AWAY; BEHOLD ALL THINGS HAVE BECOME NEW.

–2 Corinthians 5:17

New (*kainos*): saved, freshness, regenerated

Creation (*ktisis*): an original formation

Passed away (*parerchomai*): perish

Spirit (*pneuma*)		Soul (*psuche*)		Body (*soma*)
0	>	0	>	0

Old   Man   (lost)

(*palaios*)   (*antropos*)

Spirit (*pneuma*)		Soul (*psuche*)		Body (*soma*)
+	>	0	>	0

New   Man (saved)

(*kainos*)   (*antropos*)

1 Thess. 5:23; Rom. 6:3–4; Eph. 4:22, 24 (For further study)

Chart 4

Growth Stages of a Christian

1. Newborn babes (1 Pet. 2:2)
   a. Desire the sincere milk of the Word to grow
   b. Want to eat
   c. Grow rapidly
   d. Can't feed themselves
   e. Need a mother to bring things close because they can't see too far
   f. Are very trusting because everything is cozy and warm
2. Little children (I John 2:12)
   a. Must realize they are forgiven of their sins
   b. Focus on themselves and their surroundings
   c. Have more written to them
   d. Need clear and gentle repetition
   e. Are tossed to and fro with every wind of doctrine
   f. Have their cozy life upset
   g. Focus on the power of Satan
3. Young men (1 John 2:13)
   a. Have overcome the wicked one
   b. Are strong and the Word of God abides in them
4. Fathers (1 John 2:1)
   a. Have known God from the beginning
   b. Behold God's sovereignty and walk in that truth

(Printed with acknowledgment to Donna Stamey Carver for permission.)

Chart 5

Union with Christ as a Small Seed

Within the Roots of the Fruit-Bearing Tree as Portrayed by a Bible

<u>Romans 1–11</u>
DOCTRINES
Salvation: Eph. 2:8–9
Justification: Rom. 5:1
Redemption: Eph. 1:7
Sanctification: 1 Cor. 1:2,
1 Thess. 5:23
Attributes of God

<u>Romans 12–16</u>
GROWTH
2 Cor. 3:18
Col. 1:5–6
Col. 2:9–10
Phil. 1:6
Ps. 119:160
Ps. 119:11

Chart 6

Chronological Order of New Testament Books

Matthew depicted AD 30–33, written in AD 60
Mark depicted AD 30–33, written in AD 50
Luke depicted AD 30–33, written in AD 60
John depicted AD 30–33, written in AD 60

Paul saved in Acts chapter 9, around AD 35
James written in AD 40
1 Thessalonians AD 51*
2 Thessalonians AD 51*
Galatians AD 54*
1 Corinthians AD 56*
2 Corinthians AD 57*
Romans AD 58*
Acts AD 61—26:14–18 future progressive revelation to Paul
Philemon AD 61*
——**MYSTERY REVEALED**——
Ephesians AD 63*
Philippians AD 63*
Colossians AD 63*
1 Timothy AD 63*
Titus AD 65*
Hebrews AD 65
1 Peter AD 65
2 Peter AD 65
2 Timothy AD 66*
Jude AD 75
1John AD 85
2 John AD 85
3 John AD 85
Revelation AD 95 (prophetic)

*Paul's epistles

The canon of scripture was completed about AD 110.

Chart 7

Comparison of Sadducees and Pharisees

Sadducees	Pharisees
1. Aristocratic priests	Rigid realists (Scribes)
2. Legalists	Socialists
3. Acknowledged only the written law as binding Rejected entire traditional interpretation by the elders, not the prophets.	Milder and merciful
4. Strictly adhered to the letter of the law	Sought to mitigate law's severity by interpretation.
5. Rejected Pharisee rituals (clean, unclean) but demanded a higher level of cleanness for the priest who burned the red heifer.	Adhered strictly to rituals.
6. Refused to believe in a resurrection of the body and retribution in a future life or in personal continuity of the individual.	Believed in the resurrection of the body, a future life, and continuity of the individual.
7. Denied angel or spirit.	Believed in the supernatural.
8. Stressed human freedom.	Accepted God's preordination.

Chart 8

Comparison of Pharisees and Christians

Pharisees	Christians
1. Adhered to moral precepts of law	Jesus came to fulfill the law
2. Detailed law with extreme minutia	Lived by God's grace
3. Truth for speculation or entrapment	Faith is a fruit of inner man
4. Draw attention to themselves	Humility as a fruit
5. Poor class was shunned	Compassion for the poor

Chart 9

In Christ

Romans

1 Corinthians

2 Corinthians

Galatians

Ephesians

Philippians

Colossians

1 Thessalonians

2 Thessalonians

1 Timothy

2 Timothy

Philemon

Chart 10

SIN AND GROWTH

SALVATION _Sin_____
at   _____
The Cross   ____ _____

^^^^^^^^^^^^^^

_____

^^^^^^^^^^

_____

^^^^^^^

_____

_____ ^^

__

__

Glory
    of
      HEAVEN

Chart 11

CONTRAST OF LOST AND SAVED

(Rom. 8:1–14)

	Lost	Saved
1.	Walk after the flesh (8:1)	Walk after the Spirit (8:1)
2.	In bondage (8:2–3)	Free from law of sin/death (8:2–3)
3.	Unrighteous (8:4)	Righteousness of law fulfilled (8:4)
4.	Mind fleshly things. (8:5)	Mind spiritual things (8:5)
5.	Carnally minded = death (8:6)	Spiritually minded = life (8:6)
6.	God's enemy (8:7)	God's redeemed (8:7)
7.	Cannot please God (8:8)	Serve God (8:8)
8.	No indwelling Spirit (8:9)	Indwelling Spirit (8:9)
9.	Death in sin only (8:10–11)	Dead body; alive by Spirit (8:10–11)
10.	Separated from God (8:12–14)	Sons of God (8:12–14)

NOTES

Chapter 4

1. Thomas H. Everette, Lillian M. Weber, Graeme Pierce Berlyn, "Tree Structure and Growth" Encyclopaedia Britannica, last updated 11/20/2015, accessed February 4, 2017, www.Britannica.com/plant/tree/structureandgrowth.

Chapter 5

1. Carole Anderson Lucia, "20 Breastfeeding Benefits for Mom and Baby," Fit Pregnancy and Baby, accessed March 19, 2016, http://www.fitpregnancy.com/baby/breastfeeding/20–breastfeeding-benefits-mom-baby; "What Is Colostrum? How Does It Benefit My Baby?" La Leche League International, last modified January 9, 2016, accessed March 19, 2016, http://www.lalecheleague.org/faq/colostrum.html.

2. Reverend Linda Smallwood, "The names and attributes of God, My Redeemer Lives Ministry, accessed March 21, 2016, http://www.myredeemerlives.com/namesofgod/el-shaddai.html.

3. Dr Jay L Hoecker, answer to question, "How much should I expect my baby to grow in the first year? Mayo Clinic Patient Care & Health Info, Healthy Life Style, Infant and toddler health, accessed March 25, 2016, http://www.mayoclinic.org/healthy-lifestyle/infant-and-toddler-health/expert-answers/infant-growth/faq-20058037.

4. "Infant Vision: Birth to 24 Months of Age", American Optometric Association, Washington, DC, accessed April 18, 2016. http://www.aoa.org/patients-and-public/good-vision-throughout-life/childrens-vision/infant-vision-birth-to-24–months-of-age?sso=y#1

5. Roy Benaroch, MD, "Teaching children how to behave; 5 essential principles", written February 19, 2013, accessed April 23, 2016, http://www.kevinmd.com/blog/2013/02/teaching-children-behave-5–essential-principles.html.

6. Clifton Fadiman, "Children's Literature, Encyclopaedia Britannica, last updated 9/25/2015, accessed April, 24, 2016, http://www.britannica.com/art/childrens-literature.

7. "Student Well-Being, Healing Classrooms, accessed February 5, 2017, http://healingclassrooms.org/1/3/8.html

8. Barbara Morrongiello, PhD, Brae Anne McArthur, MA "Parent Supervision to Prevent Injuries", Encyclopedia on Early Child Development, accessed May 1, 2016, http://www.child-encyclopedia.com/parenting-skills/according-experts/parent-supervision-prevent-injuries.

9. Dr William Sears, "Ask Dr. Sears: Mashing Monster Fears", Parenting, accessed May 2, 2016, http://www.parenting.com/article/ask-dr-sears-mashing-monster-fears.

10. Tim Elmore, "The Marks of Maturity", Psychology Today, posted November 14, 2012, accessed May 11, 2016, https://www.psychologyto-day.com/blog/artificial-maturit

11. Keith Zafren, "Essential Fathering Skills All Dads Can Master and All Kids Need", accessed May 16, 2016, http://www.lawyerment.com/library/articles/Relationships/Children_and_Parentng/6193.htm.

12. "Initial Words of Wisdom" Dad's Adventure, accessed February 5, 2017, http://www.dadsadventure.com/becoming-a-dad/initial-words-of-wisdom/#sthash.2oK3y9yo.dpbs.

Chapter 6

1. The Red Heifer, Order of Burning the Red Heifer, The Temple Institute, accessed February 5, 2017, https://www.templeinstitute.org/red_heifer/red_heifer_contents.htm.

Made in the USA
Lexington, KY
16 September 2017